# ALLIGATOR DREAMS
*The Story of Greenwood Ridge Vineyards*

By
## RICHARD PAUL HINKLE
Photography by
## KATE KLINE MAY

GREENWOOD R

OGE VINEYARDS

*Oil pastel on paper by Martha Anne Booth.*

*Editing:* Pam D'Angelo
*Design and art direction:* Allan Green
*Production*: Victoria Hand

# Silverback Books, Inc.
1815 Fourth Street
Santa Rosa, California 95404

ISBN 1-930603-30-4

Printed in Hong Kong

# Contents

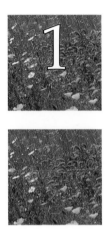

# Not by Design

If your name is not Mondavi—or Gallo, or Martini, or Pedron-celli or Wente—you do not set out, almost from birth, to become a winegrower.

Therefore, the fact that designer Allan Green did *not* set out to become a winegrower is not the least bit surprising. But, as you'll see, neither is it surprising that he ended up one. You see, the occupation "winegrower"—that is to say, someone who both grows grapes *and* shepherds their wending way on through to vinous reality—is a vastly intriguing, broadly multi-cultural, "designing," if you will, enterprise. Indeed, the largest part of wine's fascination—for consumers and professionals alike—lies in the fact that it requires such a multiplicity of interest, farsightedness and expertise, or at least willingness to learn, to expand, to grow, to be almost endlessly fascinated. And, in turn, to *become* fascinating.

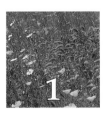

Most folk, when they get beyond the area of their "job," quickly run into shallow waters. But winegrowers, because of the inherently multi-tasking enterprise in which they are engaged, easily respond to a broad range of topics without faltering. Consider the job description. Agriculture is its broadest and most expansive base. But there's also the endless science and technology of maturing grapes with an identity, grapes with sufficient definition and character to proclaim their origins all the way into bottle, and on into a single glass. What rootstock? What clone? How do they match up with this patch of ground, slope, exposure, this particular bit of microclimate?

The actual winemaking side equally draws on science and technology, but is mightily laced with the intuitive, the artistic, the almost mystical sense of trying to understand something so fluid, so elusive, so changeable. Then, too, there's the need to employ sound business practices, the need to woo critics and public like swains, the need to market and to promote and, lastly, the need to actually *sell* the "stuff." Remember Omar Khayyam's classically rhetorical musing: "I often wonder what the Vintners buy / One half so precious as the Goods they sell." It's only fermented grape juice, I oft remind myself. At once so basic and yet so completely ethereal and wondrous.

Into this venue enters the visual designer . . . entirely by accident. Understand, we're talking serendipitous in the extreme, capital "S." And yet curiously fated in some mysterious way as well. The son of a physician and an architect (a right hand man to Frank Lloyd Wright, no less). The brother of a filmmaker. A lover, in his own right, of light and pattern, texture and touch, sensuality and music.

"My mother's parents lived in San Francisco," recounts Allan. "There were several artists on her mother's side, the Pausons. The Pauson men were great businessmen, but all the Pauson women were artistic. Jeanette Pauson Haber, my mother's mom, made most of the pottery in my house. My mother, Jean Haber Green, wove the upholstery you see over there in the living room. My great aunt, Rose Pauson, was a painter." One

of the rooms of Allan's wondrous home is devoted to the art of his great aunt. One hallway wall is given over to a colorful collection of fruit crate-end labels Allan put together in college—from orange, pear, and lemon growers—while another guest room features framed David Lance Goines posters.

"Do you remember Pauson & Co., the San Francisco men's clothiers? That's the family. They lived at 2510 Jackson Street. In 1919, the Pausons bought a five-acre apricot orchard in Los Altos, down the San Francisco Peninsula. Five dollars an acre. They later built a little house there. That's where I grew up."

Allan Green was born in Los Angeles on May 24th, 1949. His father, Aaron G. Green, had been working with Frank Lloyd Wright in both Wisconsin (Taliesin, at Spring Green) and Arizona at Taliesin West. "My mother's aunt, Rose Pauson, had hired Wright to design a house for her in Phoenix. This was in the late '30s, and my father was part of the Wright organization at the time. That's where Mom and Dad met. When Dad returned from the Air Force, they married and moved to Los Angeles."

Two years after Allan's birth, Aaron Green decided to open an office in San Francisco. It would also become the West Coast office of the Frank Lloyd Wright Foundation, with Aaron as his West Coast representative. (Wright died in 1959. Allan remembers Easter egg hunts at Taliesin West when he was a child.)

Wright designed the much lauded Marin County Civic Center; Aaron Green was responsible for construction of that landmark edifice which, in Wright's mind, was "bridging these hills with graceful arches." (Aaron Green's book explaining that soaring, "spaceship-like" structure, *An Architecture for Democracy*, was designed by Allan Green. In that book, Green reminds us of Wright's dictum that "A good building . . . is one which makes the landscape more beautiful than it was before that building was built.")

A few years after settling in San Francisco, Aaron designed an

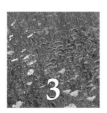

*It was Frank Green, "intrigued by the back-to-the-land movement," who spurred the family's original purchase of the rugged, forested Greenwood Ridge property.*

addition to the house in Los Altos and the family moved in. (When it was eventually sold in 1989, the five acre property was the last large undeveloped parcel in Los Altos.)

Allan graduated from Los Altos High in 1967. "I played some forgettable basketball and baseball, and painted posters," he recalls with a laugh. "I started listening to rock 'n' roll then, and it really grabbed me. I remember having to give oral presentations, and I would play rock 'n' roll on a phonograph as background music while I gave my reports." To this day, his love of music is evident in a vast and eclectic collection of CDs and the two-hour Thursday evening show he hosts for the local National Public Radio affiliate. The show is appropriately called "The Straight Ahead Rock 'n' Roll Show." Allan's theme song for the show? An obscure tune by Commander Cody and the Lost Planet Airmen whose refrain runs, "There's a whole lot of things that I've never done, and I ain't never had too much fun."

Allan spent two years at U.C. Riverside before finishing his

Bachelor's degree in art at U.C.L.A. in 1971. It was about that time that the family was looking for a weekend/summer retreat north of the Bay Area. "It was my younger brother Frank who pushed for it," Allan recounts. "The first 275 acres were purchased in 1971, and we subsequently added the vineyard property and several adjacent parcels. We've been able to reassemble about 900 acres of the original 1600-acre Berry Ranch."

Frank, a San Francisco documentary filmmaker and freelance cameraman, remembers being "angry at everything and intrigued by the 'back-to-the-land' movement. As a kid, I had always been fond of the coastal landscape. I liked redwood trees. The ridge was the first place the real estate agent took us on that 1971 trip. I looked at the spring, the blue sky, the green meadows, the symmetry of the ridgeline and said, 'Where do we sign?' I don't get up there as often as I'd like to these days, but I still love the place and offer as much moral support as I can to Allan and his winery. His Late Harvest Riesling is my favorite."

Jean Haber Green has a brisk and brittle sense of humor, and of herself. She downplays her role in the development of vineyard and winery (she shares ownership in the vineyard with her sons, but Allan owns the winery outright), but it is clear that the core of her character has been proudly passed on to her older son. It is correct to note that she wove the handsome red plaid couch upholstery—with strands of dark blue and highlights of copper—that covers with grace the living room cove of Allan's expansive, airy home (designed by Aaron). But the license plate of her Mercedes sedan, "JHG MD," reveals another side to this energetic lady. Stanford-educated ("I knew Wallace Stegner; he was as good a man as he was a writer"), she earned her degree in medicine at the University of California Medical School-San Francisco ("only because they wouldn't take women at Stanford's Medical School!") and practiced anesthesiology for 30 years.

"At U.C.S.F. I met Dr. Salvatore Lucia," Jean relates as we enjoy

the dinnertime view from the dining room of the Albion River Inn. "Dr. Lucia, as you know, was one of the first to write seriously about the myriad health benefits of wine. He was an imposing man, something of a patrician in his manner, and when he entered a classroom he had everyone's attention."

In 1971 Salvatore Pablo Lucia, M.D. published the seminal book *Wine and Your Well-Being*, in which he wrote, "Wine is a food; a source of energy for work and body maintenance. . . . Because of the tranquilizing effect of its alcohols and esters, together with the appetite-stimulating effect of its organic acids, dry table wine may be useful in overcoming lack of appetite, especially when this is caused by emotional tensions."

Long retired from medicine, Jean Haber Green lives in Palo Alto, where much of her considerable energy is expended in support of classical music programs, from Stanford University

*Jean Haber Green, in 1972, patiently anticipates that first cool drink of water from the property's new well.*

*That's Aaron Green enjoying an afternoon siesta. Too long a nap, however, can sometimes turn into a real nightmare.*

to the San Francisco Symphony. But she spends a good deal of time, especially in the summer, at her modest cabin just over the hill from the vineyard and can often be found lending a hand in the tasting room and helping out with the chocolate tasting booth at the annual California Wine Tasting Championships in July. Her bright, sparkling eyes and energetic involvement make it clear how she feels about the success of Greenwood Ridge Vineyards.

Allan was still working toward his Master's—awarded in 1974 by U.C.L.A.—in 1973 when the family bought a young vineyard, immediately adjacent to their original parcel, from Tony Husch. "We hadn't planned on growing grapes, we were just trying to preserve the peacefulness of our rural environment," says Allan in a contemplative mood.

In 1968 Tony and Gretchen Husch had purchased the Nunn Ranch, known for apples and grains, about halfway between Philo and Navarro. They knew that an apple climate was equally suitable for wine grapes. There they planted Chardonnay, Pinot Noir and Gewürztraminer and built Anderson Valley's first new winery in the modern era. (Dr. Donald Edmeades had previously planted 24 acres of *vinifera* [European wine] grapes in 1964, but the family's winery, opened by son Deron Edmeades, with Pamela DuPratt, didn't open until 1972. Allan designed the noted Edmeades labels that depicted colorful coastal Mendocino County themes.)

Tony and Gretchen wanted to produce Cabernet and Merlot, too, and that would require a warmer climate. Hence, the heavily forested 1400-foot ridge uphill from Hendy Woods State Park and Greenwood Creek, on the road to Elk—dotted by madrone, California laurel, oak, redwood, and other conifers—above Philo. There they planted three acres of own-rooted Cabernet and two-and-a-half acres each of Merlot and White Riesling in 1972. Didn't have to water much. Annual rainfall is 60 inches a year. But within a year they conceded that they might have bitten off a bit more than they could chew.

When Allan had started at U.C. Riverside, he had no major in mind. "It was the art classes that I liked the most, and that's why I transferred to U.C.L.A., for their art major. I enjoyed painting and sculpture. But the design shop was next to the sculpture lab, and I found myself gravitating there more and more. Three-dimensional product design work really got my brain kick-started. It was challenging and endlessly fascinating. I did my Master's in industrial design and graphic design."

Summers and holidays he managed to spend a good deal of time on the ridge and in the valley, making friends with Anderson Valley's vinous pioneers. "I met Tony and Gretchen in 1971. Deron Edmeades had a softball team, and I began to play with them. Still do, every Tuesday night! That's how I met all the wine people. I think Jed [Steele] came in seventy-three. The softball team was called the 'Philo Winos.' It was the major social aspect of the valley on weekends, and the games were really family affairs. Hanging out with them, I got interested in what they were doing: wine. Very interesting."

Allan had had a design studio in a cabin on the Los Altos property, and there he did design work for magazines. In 1976 he was offered the position of assistant art director at Sunset

Magazine, but by then the notion of being a grape farmer was thoroughly infecting his thinking. "One of the parcels we bought had an old woodbutcher's cabin," he recalls. "Pedro lives in it now, but it needed a lot of work back then. I remodeled it into a house I could live in by the end of that year. In 1977 I came up here to live full time, though I do have a condo in San Francisco, and I'm often there on weekends."

He had planned to make a little wine from the vineyard's first crop in 1976. That fall, when the grapes were coming into ripeness, he returned from a three-day trip to the city to find his young vines bare. "I walked out in the vineyard . . . and there was nothing! I asked the caretakers, 'What happened?' It had gotten foggy, and a flock of starlings or robins had swarmed in for a feast."

In 1977, the vineyard's first commercial crop was sold to Jed Steele, over at Edmeades. "A basketball player at Gonzaga, Jed played on our softball team. He had become my unofficial consultant. Whenever I had any questions, I'd ask Jed. In 1978, most of the Riesling and Cabernet grapes went to Edmeades again, but I held back a little Riesling to make some home wine. We actually built the first stage of our winery for my first home winemaking venture.

"I was always asking Jed, 'What do I do now?' We fermented the wine in a stainless steel drum that sat in a picking bin. We put ice in the water in the bin to keep the fermenting wine [in the drum] from getting too warm. I don't remember how we filtered the stuff, but we must have. We hand-bottled the wine, using pretty much any bottles we could corral."

The wine tasted pretty good to Allan. "We had the advantage of having a cool building. Plus, we pick so late up here that it's practically winter by the end of fermentation anyway, so it really wasn't all that difficult to keep the wine cool. Somehow, somebody convinced me to send a couple of bottles to the Orange County Fair's home winemaking competition. It won a gold medal. I thought, 'Hey, this is easy. Anybody can do this!' I was a winemaker."

# Starting a Winery

A successful first decade is vital to a new winery's existence. It's easy to fail. The competition is high, and the quality bar is constantly being raised to heights that stagger the imagination and tantalize the palate. It's exciting for consumers, almost a nightmare for producers. Getting good, and then improving upon your successes, is a challenge and then some.

We need to set the record straight, early on in this history, that the winery's name is not a meld of Allan's last name and that of the Greens' first caretaker of the property (Steve Wood). The name came to the land from one of the first white men to map these high, wind-swept ridgelines at a time when mere fog as meteorological challenge must have looked pretty darned good. His name was Caleb Greenwood, and by the time he gave his name to the town we now know as Elk (it was initially dubbed Greenwood), he was a grizzled hunter-trapper and

wagon train "pilot." In his eighties when he led wagon trains to California—all seven of his children by his Crow wife Batchicka were sired after he turned sixty—he was widely known as "Old Greenwood." He was routinely described as being over six feet tall, raw-boned and "spare of flesh," active, a skilled marksman; "his powers of falsification were quite phenomenal; to say that he was an habitual liar would mislead, as leaving room for the inference that he sometimes spoke the truth." (This might be an exaggeration, in that Caleb was known as a "yarn teller," one who would happily lead on tenderfoots with tall tales. One letter-writer glibly, almost reverentially referred to him as "an old mountaineer, well stocked with falsehoods.")

Each summer and fall of 1844-46 Caleb Greenwood—along with his sons, John and Britton—led convoys of Conistoga covered wagons across the heartland of our country to the land called California, as yet a wild, fecund and independent slab of raw real estate. A shortcut, south of Bear Lake and northeast of the Great Salt Lake, was known to westward emigrants as the "Greenwood Cutoff." While Caleb was said to have led the first wagon train across the Sierra Nevada Mountains (diverted by Caleb from its original destination in Oregon), and founded the town that took his name for a time, Caleb may be best remembered for organizing the second Donner relief party in 1847. But locally "Old Greenwood" is most known for offering his good name to town, creek and ridge. (There is also a Greenwood Valley in El Dorado County, where he settled for a time during the Gold Rush years.) He had no way of knowing, in those perilous times, that his name would end up being tied to wines highly distinctive of their upland regional identity.

Possibly the first white settler to the area was Francisco Faria, who lived for a time with Indians, was once mauled by a wounded bear, married and became a saloonkeeper. He was known locally as "Portagee" Frank. Born in the Azores in February of 1799, Faria had the distinction of having lived in three centuries when he died in October 1904.

Logging, for the longest time, identified the south ridges above the Anderson Valley and much of the Mendocino coast. By 1882 there were no less than twenty sawmills between Usal and Gualala. Ingenious "tinker toy" lumber chutes were designed to transfer huge logs to "lumber schooners" brought in close to shore. In 1890 the Elk Creek Railroad was built to more efficiently move cut timber to the shore for transport. But there were sharp curves and steep grades, and it was a tenuous, dangerous business from beginning to end.

It was simple economics, and perhaps a *soupçon* of pride, that pushed Green from grape grower to "winegrower." As he relates it, "The question was really quite simple: Could I support myself on grape sales? The answer to that was No. The next question was, Could I support myself if I made wine from our grapes? The answer there was in the affirmative."

There was another reason, in the end. Once he and Jed began making the wines they discovered that the Ridge had something clear and powerful to say in terms of wine identity, in terms of wine personality. In brief, wines off of the ridgeline were distinctive. They had that special personality of place that marks the world's greatest wines, from the velvet texture of Burgundy to the violet scents of Pauillac.

(There is also a five-acre plot of apples, almost adjacent to the winery. "They're probably eighty or ninety years old, and only give a crop once every other year," notes Allan. "We made a little wine from them in 1980. It wasn't very good—pretty high in acid.")

## First wine

From its very first commercial wine, Greenwood Ridge Vineyards started out a winner. Upon its release in 1981, at just $6.75 the bottle, the 1980 White Riesling was acclaimed for its crisp, lemon-filled, Germanic styling. Anthony Dias Blue, writing in the *San Francisco Chronicle*, gushed over the wine. "[It] displays a smooth and classic Riesling nose and greets the tongue with lemony fruit and classic Teutonic restraint." (This,

*Since the vineyard is only six miles from the ocean, it rarely snows on Greenwood Ridge, perhaps once every year or two.*

of course, from a man who once described a Ventana Chardonnay as displaying "prismatic luminescence.")

"We also made a little Cabernet that first year, but it wouldn't be ready to sell for about three years," says Allan. "So we became known as a White Riesling winery initially, and that impression held for quite a while."

The fact of the matter is that the wine was beautifully structured to last, its mineral-based fruit forming a sturdy spine. It is, to this day, a stunning example of near-dry Riesling, still straw yellow in color and perfectly vibrant and alive with apricot and lemon fruit and an oily texture that tantalizes your tongue. The wine took a gold medal at the Orange County Fair in 1981, and a silver at the Los Angeles County judging (where only one gold was awarded and the *Wine Spectator* headlined "L.A. County judges stingy with awards.") "I almost didn't enter the wines," recalls Green with a laugh, "but some friends persuaded me to give it a shot." While winning medals is not the *ne plus ultra* of recognition, it is, as Charlie Brown once so sagely counseled, "nice to be recognized in one's own lifetime."

Actually getting the winery running involved a year or so of craziness. "My last amateur wine, the 1979 Riesling, turned out to be very bitter, perhaps from a sulphur dioxide overdose," grumbles Green. "I had realized that I couldn't pursue my career in graphic design from up here on the Ridge. But I also

14

knew that, while an eight-acre vineyard wasn't going to make a career, a small winery based on that eight-acre vineyard could. And I thought what Anderson Valley needed was wineries, not just more vineyards.

"It was a hectic time. We had all that paperwork to complete for the state and federal authorities to get our winery bonded in August of 1980. I had met a girl, Karen Meek, we had moved up here, and we had gotten married in August. We didn't have a party. We just went to Reno. We decided to have the party afterward."

"Afterward" ended up being July of 1981. But by the time the invitations got to the printer, Karen had left. "I had to call the printer, have our names deleted, and call it the 'First Anniversary of the Winery' party."

For the most part, the winery's expansion came in small, orderly increments. The first section—1000 square feet of cinder block, tucked into the slope above the vineyard pond—was raised in 1978. The siding came from fallen redwood trees on the property. The shake roof angled off in different directions, but the basics were lots of drainpipe and lots of silver-sided insulation. Grapes were dumped into the crusher-stemmer from plastic buckets.

"We had a two-bottle hand filler to bottle our wines, and a small, hand-cranked basket press," says Allan with the laugh of someone comfortable to have progressed to far better, far less labor-intensive equipment. "Today, when we bottle, we hire a mobile bottling crew. They have a 25 foot Isuzu Turbo truck that houses a state-of-the-art bottling line.

"They just back that big truck right in on our pad next to the pond, we hook up lines from our tanks to their filler . . . and we can bottle half our production in two days!" In the old days, bottling crews were fueled with lots of the *cerveza* (there's an old saying, "It takes a lot of beer to make good wine!"), but these days, what with liability concerns and a healthy dose of common sense, Allan stocks up on cases of ice-cold Coca Cola®.

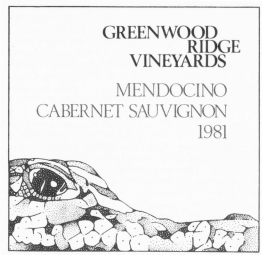

GREENWOOD
RIDGE
VINEYARDS

MENDOCINO
CABERNET SAUVIGNON
1981

Grown, produced and bottled by Greenwood Ridge Vineyards,
B.W. 4960, Philo, California. Alcohol 12.5% by volume.

*You can see how the ridgeline (left) inspired Allan's original "alligator" label.*

Somehow, the bottling line runs a bit smoother on caffeine than on alcohol.

## Alligator dreams

It's as important to have a label that draws attention (to incite that vital first taste) as it is to have wines of sufficient character to bring consumers back for their second (and third) taste. It was on my first visit to the winery, in August of 1982, that Allan explained the evolution of his label design.

"Our initial label began, in my mind, as a drawing of the skyline of the adjacent ridge," explained Allan, then still in his designer mode. "Somehow, it morphed on its own into an alligator's head. It turned out to be, on another level entirely, something of a parody on those with vineyard sites on rich, bottom land. Our soils are thin and rocky. We'd kiddingly say, 'Half crocked.' Crocodile? Alligator? It's a bad pun, I know. But somehow, it just worked. People remembered it. 'Oh, you're the one with the alligator!' It kind of had a life of its own." Much later he would acknowledge, "We're going to bring it back, in one form or another." One of the gator's reincarnations came in 1999, in the form of a dragon, on the chocolate label. But there could be something else in the offing. It's too good of a story to let lay fallow. Plus, it's just too much fun, and Allan's pretty good at latching on to "fun."

16

## Not just a pretty face

Tall and lean, with dark hair, hazel-brown eyes, and a neatly trimmed mustache, Allan has always had something of a professional model's look. Indeed, the March 1983 issue of *San Francisco Magazine* included Green in "The Bay Area's 100 Most Eligible Men," along with cover boy Dwight Clark of the 49ers, Giant Chili Davis, and a fellow actually named Stanley Kowalski ("Stella!!") who admitted that his favorite author was, yes, Tennessee Williams.

In the magazine profile, Allan commented on the correlation between design and winemaking, saying that "in both cases you start out with raw material—an idea or some grapes—and you work it all the way through until you have a product people can enjoy. It's fun to walk into a nice restaurant and see bottles of your wine on the table. I feel like going up to people and saying, 'Hi! How do you like it?'"

## Expansion . . . and basketball

In 1981 a large basket press was acquired, greatly easing the difficult job of separating juice from solids. The following year, the largest component of the winery was built just east of the original cellar, this an 1800-square foot warehouse and bottling cellar.

In 1983 the coastal fog brought *botrytis* to the Riesling. "The 'noble mold' infected about a third of our Riesling grapes," recalls Allan. "We picked the unaffected fruit first, for our regular Riesling, and about three weeks later we picked enough fully infected fruit to make 130 gallons of sweet—thirty Brix—juice, from what had originally been four tons of fruit [enough to make more than *600 gallons* of wine from un-dehydrated grapes]. This precious juice was fermented cold and the fermentation stopped when the alcohol reached seven-point-five percent. The residual sugar at this point was over fifteen. We sterile filtered the wine to remove the remaining yeast cells and bottled it in 375-milliliter bottles. It was similar to a German *beerenauslese*, with the aromas of peaches, apricots and honey,

and quite lush in the mouth. We were thrilled to have made so lovely a sweet wine, and still are when weather conditions allow it."

Near what was then the bottling area—now casegoods storage and site of the Tasting Championships—is a basketball hoop. "I love basketball," says Allan, whose lean, spare build works well for the game. "It gives the crew incentive to get the wines bottled and labeled so that we can get on to the important stuff . . . the game! It's also something to do while pressing grapes. Kind of a relief valve." It also cost Allan a severed Achilles tendon in 1984. Ouch!

"That was quite a year, 1984," he says wistfully. "Basketball did me in physically, but a lot of good things happened on the wine side. We had a large Merlot crop, so much that we decided to make our first varietal Merlot that year. We didn't quite realize just how good a wine it was going to make up here. Our Riesling was doing very well, winning all those medals. When my assistant, Kevin Orr, left to manage his wife's dental practice, I knew that I needed some help in the cellar. As good as our 1980 Riesling turned out, I still remembered that '79. And as many U.C. Davis Extension classes as I had taken on grape growing and winemaking, I still didn't feel that I had sufficient background.

"I put an ad in the paper and found a guy who grew up taking care of his family's vineyard [next door to Silver Oak], had a degree from U.C. Davis, and work experience at Fieldstone Winery in Alexander Valley. It was Fred Scherrer. I remember having my final interview with Fred, out in the vineyard; I was on crutches. My Achilles had just been sewed back together. It became apparent to me that he knew a lot more than I did, plus he had all that experience to draw on. So, in the spring of 1985 I turned the day-to-day winemaking and vineyard supervision over to Fred."

Fred remembers the experience as being "a lot of work, but Allan was easy to work for, so laid back, so casual, and very generous. I remember when he lent my girlfriend his Corvette.

**18**

It was a big deal to her. I especially liked working with cellarman Ronnie Karish. For all his apparent goofing around, he has a very colorful, very understanding interpretation of life."

In a way, Green got two-for-one when he hired Scherrer. Not only did Fred bring his knowledge and experience to bear in drawing out the best from the fruit being grown on the Ridge, but when the winery began bringing in some Scherrer Vineyards Zinfandel, it added a wine that quickly became a hallmark for the variety.

"It was in 1986 that we made our first Zinfandel from Scherrer Vineyards, perhaps three or four tons of fruit," says Green. "Fred had always wanted to make some wine from his father's grapes, so I said, Why not? Let's try it. When Fred left before the 1988 harvest to go to Dehlinger—his girlfriend [now wife, Judi] lived in Berkeley, and she got tired of driving to Philo— we were lucky enough to still get some of the vineyard's fruit. Now that Fred's started his own label, I just hope that he doesn't get so big that he needs all that fruit. But I'll be happy to get what grapes I can get from him as long as I can get them.

19

They're wonderful, and they've really helped put us on the map."

## A place to taste

Allan hadn't initially considered having a tasting room on Highway 128. But it would have been impossible to expect people to drive the six miles of winding road above Hendy Woods State Park even though the zoning would have allowed an on-site tasting room. Not to mention the large scale imposition on his personal privacy.

In 1985 a seven-acre triangular patch of land adjacent to the Navarro Vineyards tasting room (and across the street from Edmeades Vineyards) came on the market. "The land had an ugly, eyesore mobile home on it." assesses Allan. "But it was a *prominent* eyesore. The property had long highway frontage that offered great visibility from both sides, so the site certainly had great potential for a tasting room. I had known the owner a little bit. He had moved to Illinois. So I phoned him. His first response was, 'Didn't you used to date my daughter?' Damn!"

A deal was worked out, and Allan immediately turned his

*The tasting room as seen from Highway 128's western approach.*

20

architect father, Aaron Green, loose on the project. The elder
Green came up with an octagonal pyramid, with a sweeping,
encircling deck that opens up to an expansive sheep and vine-
laced view of the valley, a pond ("used to be a swamp"), and
a wind row of poplars along the northeastern edge of the
property planted by the folks next door at Navarro Vineyards.
A bridge crosses the pond to a small island with extra picnic
tables. The tasting room itself was all built from a single,
massive redwood that had fallen on the Ridge property some
twenty years before.

On Memorial Day 1986 the handsome tasting room opened to
visitors, who can view a small part of Allan's wine can collection

*This aerial view shows the triangular tasting room parcel looking east. That's next
door Navarro Vineyards to the upper left.*

*This photograph by Richard Gillette of the tasting room in early spring originally appeared in Heidi Cusick's book* Mendocino.

(now approaching 375 different wine cans), sample available wines, and purchase logo T-shirts, wine glasses, a novel written by one tasting room host (Connie Wallace, right in top photo, with colleague Teresa Simon), a "Hawaiian Motown" CD by another (Patrice Ka'ohi, right photo), and a variety of wine collectibles (including Allan's unique gift pack that brings together wine, art and music, more on which in the next chapter). More than 25,000 wine lovers drop by each year—on their way to and from the rugged, scenic Mendocino Coast—to take in the view, picnic, sample Allan's wines, and stock their cellars.

(The very existence of Greenwood Ridge Vineyards Sauvignon Blanc is a direct off-shoot of having the tasting room. "Well, we figured that we needed a dry white wine to sell there," says Green with an embarrassed laugh. "It wasn't enough to just

*The unique octagonal geometry of the tasting room structure is dramatically portrayed from this vantage point directly overhead.*

*To provide access to picnic tables on the island Aaron Green designed this enticing bridge, which was added to the tasting room environs in 1998.*

offer White Riesling and Cabernet. For a couple of years, we got Jed Steele, then with Kendall-Jackson, to make a little Sauvignon Blanc for our label.")

## End of the decade

In 1986 the Greenwood Ridge Vineyards Cabernet Sauvignon 1982 won "Best of Class" at the California State Fair Wine Competition. Where the first year's output of the winery had been less than 600 cases, production was now up to 3000 cases a year (almost half of what it is today).

When Fred left, Allan once again placed newspaper ads, this time lighting upon a Fresno State grad who had been cellar-master at the vaunted Chateau Montelena (one of that winery's early Chardonnays had won the widely heralded Paris Tasting of 1976, toppling the best the French had to offer). Van

Williamson, now winemaker at nearby Edmeades Estate (a Kendall-Jackson property), turned out to be the right man at the right time.

"I turned the winemaking over to Van and focused my efforts on marketing and sales," says Green. "We made Merlot again, as a varietal for only the second time. Before, we had blended it with our Cabernet. As you know, it turned out pretty well."

26

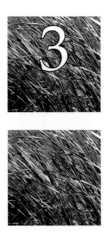

# Developing the Line

The 1890s may have been "gay" a century ago. The decade of the 1990s certainly didn't start out unhappily on the Ridge either. Right out of the chute, at the 1990 Reno West Coast Wine Competition, Greenwood Ridge Vineyard's 1989 Sauvignon Blanc was voted the "Best White Wine" award. (More on awards below.)

While many critics pointed to winemaker Van Williamson as the source of Greenwood Ridge Vineyards' increasing success in the marketplace, Williamson himself pointed to the vineyards as being the starting place for wine identity and quality. Williamson had started his college career at Chico State, looking to a career in engineering. When he transferred to Fresno State, the lure was wine. "I figured I could either be an average engineer or an outstanding winemaker," he said. After his graduation in 1984, he worked at Fetzer Vineyards and Chateau Montelena before coming to Mendocino's mountains.

One thing Van liked at Greenwood Ridge was the wild mushroom hunting. "There's a spot just below Frank's house that's the best place I've ever found," he says with enthusiasm. Also a good place to grow grapes? "Absolutely. A regular 'banana belt,' a temperate zone, being above the fog and all. Not too hot, not too cold. The only difficulty is the Cabernet. It's a struggle getting it ripe. That's the hard one to make up there, but when it does get ripe, is it good! The Merlot is classic, all perfume with those plum, raspberry and floral notes. Almost any variety that you can get mature up there will be unique. I think the apple orchard—it's the warmest spot on the property—would be ideal for Zinfandel.

"I have to say, too, that my extensive interest in fine, imported beers has certainly enhanced my career as a winemaker." We're not sure whether he's in deadly earnest, or just pulling our leg, but the wines he's making at Edmeades Estate today further confirm his aim toward the status of "outstanding winemaker." Van made the move to Edmeades from Greenwood Ridge in 1994, turning the winemaking reins over to Allan once again.

## Music and art: wine suites

The product of a complex co-mingling of many disciplines—from agriculture to science, from art to technology—wine equally appeals to a multitude of our senses.

When asked almost daily to describe his wines, Allan gradually began to find disabling paucity in mere verbal descriptions. Especially when teaching his "Introduction to California Wines" class at Mendocino Community College he noted the difficulty with "wine words," wondering if art or music might offer other means of insight. Frustrated, he began to explore these other means of description.

"Over the years," he explains, "I have found that when trying to describe the taste and aroma of a wine I often see a visual image before any words come to mind. From this experience, I became intrigued with the idea of using music and art as a new language to describe wine to others. It seemed to me that people with musical or artistic abilities might be able to give us new images of wine."

As early as 1987 he began to put his thoughts to the test, further expanding our understanding of wine in an artistic context. Green commissioned three visual and two musical artists to interpret three of his wines: the White Riesling, the Sauvignon Blanc and the Cabernet Sauvignon. The results were packaged so that one bottle of each wine could be purchased with a cassette tape of the musical compositions and color reproductions of each of the nine paintings that were the culmination of this innovative approach.

Artist Toni Littlejohn at first wondered if this was just another fancy ploy for a commercial, but was reassured that it was only her artistic reaction that was requested. Littlejohn employed oil, pastel and collage, working on paper in a sweepingly light, airy fashion. "The Riesling was interesting, giving off a feeling of ecstasy, something bubbly, light. What I saw, from each of the wines, were doorways, windows, entryways. The Riesling's window is majestic, light and airy. The Cabernet enters through a big doorway, with the rush of waves and the heady strength

*Toni Littlejohn's bright, airy "Window" for White Riesling. Oil, pastel and collage on paper, the original is 18 x 22 inches.*

of red."

Nancy Willis used oil and pastel, also on paper. From her point of view, Riesling's "window" exhibits yellows and greens, while Cabernet's "door" elicits far darker, almost sinister shades of brown and black.

*Nancy Willis' brooding "Cabernet Sauvignon." Oil and pastel on paper, the original is 18 inches square. On the opposite page, top, Nancy's interpretation of Sauvignon Blanc, and below is her artistic impression of White Riesling.*

Sauvignon Blanc

Wynne Hayakawa, working in oil on canvas, chose bright yellows and oranges for her two Rorschachian white wine paintings, shifting to reds and blues to depict Cabernet Sauvignon as something of a two-toned mushroom. (Or does that bluish object represent an eyeball into the vinous world?)

"I'm not sure, either," admits Allan. "What I do know is that they are personal interpretations of the aromas and flavors of the three wines. The similarities in the paintings of these very different artists indicate, to me at least, that sampling a wine does create a visual picture, as well as a taste sensation."

On the musical side, composer/pianist John Sergeant's *Wine Suites* describes the total wine tasting experience, from the wine splashing into one's glass to the lively play of the wine as it dances across one's tongue. Sergeant says he spent a few

*"Sauvignon Blanc" by Wynne Hayakawa. The oil on canvas original is 30" x 24".*

weeks working with the wines before he sat down at his piano and reacted to each wine, often with a glass in hand as he puttered at the keys. A collector of wine, he says that his aural impression begins with the splash of wine entering the glass, followed by his "taste buds waking up to the wine."

For the Sauvignon Blanc, Sergeant's rich, resonant synthesizer major chords evoke images of Eden, while for Cabernet he employs bass-driven glissandos substantial enough to be the theme for a TV cowboy epic. (All I could think of, listening to this piece, was rare filet mignon and "Pass the steak sauce.") As enticing as that piece was, Sergeant's reaction to the Riesling seemed to come the closest to truly evoking the wine, with its florid piano arpeggios and Italianesque "gondola music," peppered with American "rag" impressions. Lively and inclusive, just like the wine.

*Looking Through the Glass* are three compositions by violinist/composer Mark Volkert, then assistant concertmaster of the San Francisco Symphony. The Sauvignon Blanc piece features a tight, flitting-about violin and a languid clarinet. For the Riesling, Volkert has a wandering, humorous violin/piano duet that is puckishly reminiscent of Sergei Prokofiev's beloved "Peter and the Wolf." In his paean to the Cabernet, he turns dramatic, with a full-throated piece that might also be construed as a movie theme.

"To me," says Allan, "his three compositions reflect the complexity of the wines that he interprets musically as lightness, piquancy and a lingering richness. I'm convinced that this experiment linking wine to music and art was quite a success: I found that viewing the paintings and listening to the music while tasting the wines did expand my sensory horizons in a way that went beyond words. I suppose, being so close to these wines, that I might be getting a stronger image than most, but I do think that most anyone can get in touch with the sensations in the music and in the art that are clearly drawn from the wines."

Green first presented this unique meld of images, music and wine to the public in April 1989 at Stanford University's Hoover House at an event benefiting the Stanford Music Guild. The event was well-attended and highly praised.

(*Wine Notes and Brush Strokes*, available at the tasting room, includes the three wines, a cassette tape of the music, and color reproductions of all nine paintings.)


## It helps that the wines are good

Having been intimately involved in the wine judging gambit, I don't spend a lot of time pouring over wine competition compilations of medals. I'm far more apt to be impressed by the review of a single commentator, especially when I can handicap his or her bias to get to what I know will impress me. Robert Parker, for example, clearly favors larger-than-life red wines, made from ultra-ripe grapes and lathered with layers and layers of new French oak. Not my style, but in reading his sensory impressions I can easily extrapolate from his likes to my own. And that is far more useful than the mere like/dislike judgment extended by any panel, no matter how well made up.

That said, when a winery—especially a winery as small and as far removed from 'the action' (read "Sonapanoma") as Greenwood Ridge Vineyards is—consistently pulls down top medals from wine competitions far and wide, you kind of have to stand up and take notice. When the '89 Sauvignon Blanc knocks down four golds and two silvers on the 1990 circuit, you start tasting the wine for serious. When the '88 Merlot wins the "New World Grand Championship" it confirms what you tasted in the glass the week before, and when the '89 Pinot Noir's lascivious texture and filet-like sensuality bring home the hardware on the 1991 judging swing, you salute smartly and say "I told you so!" In 1995, the '92 Cab would take "Best of Show" at the Los Angeles County Fair.

It's at times like that that you enjoy reading the heartfelt, top

*A serene, springtime look at the winery from the western edge of the vineyard.*

*Allan Green*

marks appraisal given the 1990 Late Harvest White Riesling by your respected colleagues at *Connoisseurs' Guide to California Wine*: "Now this is what young botrytised wines should be like. The very first impressions in the nose are of deep, ripe, rich, vibrant fruit combining peaches, pears, melons and pineapples with hints of sweet lemon blossoms also evident. Neatly attached to the perky aromatic beginnings are smells of honey, almonds, tea and vanilla—in all a most inviting opening.

"On the palate, the wine nears perfection in its classic array of youthfully bright and gorgeous fruit components, its rich, honeyed viscosity, its pert acidity and its background of complexing agents. And like the late harvest Riesling of Germany, after which all the wines on these pages are fashioned, this one will get better and better with patient cellaring."

If *I* had written something so blatantly flattering, you'd be wise to check your wallet pocket or purse, but the wine *was* incredibly flush with fruit and botrytis when it first came out, and to this day it shows a fair amount of brown sugar and syrupy, Fuji apple fruit, though the 1989 (kiwi and apricot) and 1995 (apricot and honeysuckle) from that generation are aging only slightly more gracefully, still bright and balanced and loaded with fruit.

35

By 1992 winery production had expanded to nearly 6000 cases a year. That year the 1990 Scherrer Zinfandel nabbed "Best Red Wine" at the San Francisco National Wine Competition and a year later the next vintage locked up the 63rd slot in the *Wine Spectator's* Top 100 Wines of the Year. In 1996 the 1994 Scherrer Zin also made the magazine's Top 100. In '99 the 1998 White Riesling snagged "Best White" at the Mendocino County Fair.

When that much attention is paid to so small a producer, it becomes patently clear that they're getting pretty darned good fruit, year in and year out. Whether it's the Scherrer Zin (one of the most decorated vineyard designate wines on a regular basis), the Anderson Valley Sauvignon Blanc, the DuPratt Chardonnay, the supple, fleshy Pinot Noir, or the Greenwood Ridge Estate Merlot, Cabernet or White Riesling, their reception by press and public has resounded loud and clear down the halls of winedom. These are wines made from distinctive fruit, fruit that has not been diminished in its handling by a handful of great-care-taking winemakers over a period of two solid decades. Yes, the wines with the copper capsule have built up a pretty fair record to stand upon.

# Islands above the Fog

An aerial viewpoint is often the best way to see our home turf. We gain, first, a perspective that is encompassing and embracing rather than linear. On the ground, the planet seems decidedly cluttered, busy, filled to the gills with strip malls, houses and neon signs. But in the air, above and removed from the bustle of the daily push, the earth takes on a softer focus. First, there is more open space than we could have imagined from our pedestrian perspective. Far more open space. The land seems positively empty. Second, there is a continuity that is not available from the cheap seats. When you can see the curvature of the earth, there is a connectedness that you can get no other way.

It is that connectedness that applies meaning to the Mendocino Ridge appellation, placed on the register of American wine appellations in October 1997. On a map, the ridgelines and

*Mendocino ridgetops become islands above a summer's morning fog.*

mountain peaks seem fractured and far apart. But seen from the air on a normal summer's morning, when fog renders the valley an ocean floor, these high points rise up a connected archipelago and, bingo-presto, there is unity and form!

## Wine appellations

Appellations of origin are curious entities. We want them to be automatic indices of quality, but the cold, cruel fact is that they are usually slight statements of some geographical commonality (or worse, purely a political convenience).

Take Mendocino County, for instance. The appellation "Mendocino County" is a good example of political convenience. It exists, for wine consumers, merely to alert them that the grapes come from a more limited, more recognizable area than from the whole of the Golden State. That is, to be honest, some help, in that it eliminates the possibility that the grapes were grown in the blistering heat of, say, the San Joaquin Valley. (Well, almost eliminates it. In truth some fruit from areas other than the listed appellation can be blended into the wine. But only the most unscrupulous would be so brazen as to mix Central Valley fruit with coastal fruit.)

Still, Mendocino County takes in such disparate regions as Ukiah Valley (rather warm) and the western end of Anderson Valley (cool to downright chilly). That could decidedly cause a bit of confusion. Which is why more specific appellations—Anderson Valley, Redwood Valley, Potter Valley, Cole Ranch, Yorkville Highlands and McDowell Valley—serve a modestly useful purpose in giving consumers more information about, at least, the wines grown there and their stylistic differences. Chardonnays grown in the warm climate of McDowell Valley (nigh unto Lake County, in the southeastern corner of Mendocino County) are going to be bigger, more alcoholic, more lush in style than those grown in the cool, western reaches of Anderson Valley, where the wines decidedly tilt toward the lean, the crisp and the ageably austere.

The county's most recent appellation, or (the federal government's term) "American Viticultural Area" (AVA), is also its most unique. In fact, without fear of sliding into hyperbole, it may be the only appellation of origin on the third planet that may reliably be called unique at all. For "Mendocino Ridge" is unlike any other wine site on this earth in that it is *discontinuous*. It is a series of ridges and peaks whose identity is based on altitude and not on contiguousness.

Any vinous appellation worth its salt is driven by the fruit quality of its best vineyards, and in this regard Mendocino Ridge has a leg up on its competitors. The distinctive black-pepper spiced Zinfandels produced—initially by Jed Steele, later by Kendall-Jackson and others—from the likes of DuPratt, Zeni, Mariah and Ciapusci vineyards, are known, even revered wines. The crisp, flinty, long-lived White Rieslings produced here by Greenwood Ridge Vineyards have a modest, near cultish following among those inured of Germany's greatest contribution to the world of wine.

## Where Zinfandel is king

As good as the Riesling is, Zinfandel is clearly the leading light on the Mendocino Ridge. Jed Steele, writing on "Coastal Ridge Zinfandel" in 1995, expressed it this way: "That certain grape varieties, grown in specific geographical locations, produce distinctive wines that are sought after by appreciators of fine wine is a given phenomenon in the world of viticulture and enology. Illustrations of such situations are Pinot Noir when grown in Burgundy, White Riesling when grown in the Mosel Valley of Germany, and Cabernet Sauvignon when grown in the Rutherford-Oakville region of the Napa Valley. Zinfandel, when grown in the Coastal range of Mendocino County, roughly between the points where the Navarro River and Gualala River empty into the ocean, is in my mind such a classic match of grape variety with a particular climate, one that leads to the ultimate in winemaking fruit."

"We're primarily known for being a Zinfandel area," says Point Arena's Dan Dooling, owner of the famed Mariah Vineyard. "Jed Steele was a teacher's assistant at U.C. Davis when I was there, and he was the one who told me that Zinfandel would produce unique wines up here on the ridges. Initially, I sold all my Zinfandel to Jed. I grow Syrah and Merlot up here, too. We're the highest vineyard in the appellation, going up to nearly 2800 feet, and we can see the Pacific from our upper vineyard, which is just six miles from the ocean."

## The making of the appellation

Dooling and Steve Alden—who farms Zinfandel and Merlot at Alden Ranch on Fish Rock Road (one of the southeasternmost within the new appellation, along with neighbors Zeni, Ciapusci and Gianoli)—were the prime instigators of the Mendocino Ridge appellation, a concept that caused great consternation among the federal regulators, who initially rejected their application out-of-hand. They had never come across an application based on altitude rather than a wholly connected flat-land surface.

Dooling and Alden were aided in their quest by Allan Green (Greenwood Ridge Vineyards is the only winery presently

Elk

Greenwood Road

Hwy. 128

Navarro River

**GREENWOOD RIDGE VINEYARDS**

**DU PRATT VINEYARD**

Philo

Anderson Valley

Boonville

Hwy. 253

Manchester

Mountain View Road

**MARIAH VINEYARD**

Point Arena

Hwy. 1

to Cloverdale

Hwy. 128

**ALDEN RANCH**

Fish Rock Road

**ZENI VINEYARD**

**GIANOLI RANCH**

**CIAPUSCI VINEYARD**

N

Area above
1200 feet

Gualala

*Islands in the Clouds...*

# MENDOCINO RIDGE

*You can see how the vineyards unfolded, the first plantings near the winery (upper right), the later plantings draped across the ridgetop to the east.*

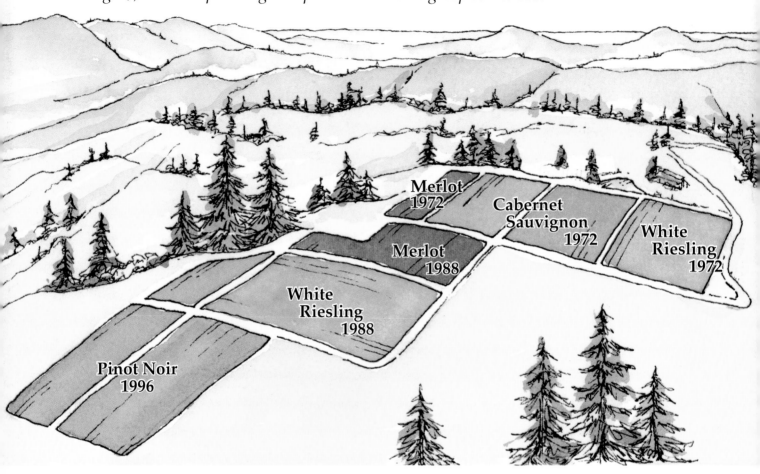

Merlot 1972

Cabernet Sauvignon 1972

White Riesling 1972

Merlot 1988

White Riesling 1988

Pinot Noir 1996

situated within the new appellation), Tom Krig (owner of the famed DuPratt Vineyard, known not only for Zinfandel, but for excellent, full-textured Chardonnay), and veteran ridge-line farmers Nick Ciapusci and the late George Zeni, a pair of names known and hailed by Zinfandel lovers far and wide. More than half of the vines planted in the new AVA are Zinfandel, with a smattering of Merlot, Cabernet Sauvignon, Syrah, Pinot Noir, Chardonnay and White Riesling.

"We formed the Mendocino Ridge Quality Alliance to petition the BATF for our own appellation in 1994," recalls Alden, under whose name the petition was formally filed. "They just returned it to us at the beginning. They had never seen anything like this before. But we just kept going back to them, showing them the weather we all shared—because of altitude—the similarity of the soils, the topographical commonalities, and the history of grape growing in this area."

*This aerial photograph, showing year-old Pinot Noir vines in the lower left corner, was taken in the summer of 1997. Note the fog layer at the Pacific's edge (top).*

This new AVA encompasses a group of ridges (including Campbell Ridge, Greenwood Ridge, McGuire Ridge, Phelps Ridge, Signal Ridge and Zeni Ridge) and mountain peaks (including Cold Spring Mountain, Gualala Mountain, Lookout Mountain and Red Rock Mountain) that rest above the 1200-foot (above mean sea level) contour line. (Of the quarter million acres [262,400 acres, to be more precise] that lie within the overall map's perimeter of the appellation, exactly one-third lie above the defining—for wine—contour line. In October 1997 only 86 of those acres were planted to the vine.)

The key to the identity of this appellation is that these are sites normally above the fog line. "The Bureau of Alcohol, Tobacco and Firearms [the federal sanctioning body] actually wanted to include the low ground between the ridges, to make a nice, clean line on their maps," says the dark-haired, one-time truck driver Dooling with a scornful laugh. "We kept explaining that the low ground wasn't the same, for grapes. That those were cooler locations, longer under the influence of the morning fog. That the whole point of this new appellation is that these are sites above the fog line, and that different varieties flourish here than down below."

Dooling notes that it took more than three years to secure the agency's final approval, "on a project that should have taken six months." Laughs Alden, "I suppose they saw us as just a bunch of hick farmers." Indeed, it took the regulators a while to recognize the subtle sophistication behind the concept. But once they did, the Mendocino Ridge would become a truly unique AVA.

## History on the vine

It was important that Alden and Dooling be able to point to some historical evidence of grape growing in the region.

*The only Cabernet Sauvignon in the Mendocino Ridge appellation, these Cabernet vines at Greenwood Ridge Vineyards were planted in 1972.*

Perspective is important in understanding historical imperatives. It is, for example, mind-tweaking to know that, on the day General George Armstrong Custer underwent his ultimate battle on the Little Bighorn River (on 26 June 1876), the Chicago White Sox defeated the Cincinnati Redstockings 3-2. At the same time, Italian settlers were peeling tan bark along the Mendocino ridges and putting cuttings of Zinfandel, Alicante-Bouschet, Carignane, Muscat, Palomino and Malvasia into the ground in an effort to instill a little of their homeland onto their new land.

Note that these are sun-worshipping varieties, none of which would have flourished down in the fog-washed lowlands. Old timers cite family names like a litany of warm pasta, tomato sauce and wine: Luccinetti, Pearli, Gianoli, Ciapusci, Soldani and Zeni homesteaded and planted vines along Fish Rock Road. Along Greenwood Ridge the names included Frati, Tovani, Guisti, Pronsolino and Giovanetti. Best guesses on acreage there prior to Prohibition? Some 150 acres along Fish Rock Road, and another 250 acres along Greenwood Ridge. Maybe.

"Three of those original vineyards have survived Prohibition," says Alden, "and at least three of the original ones had wineries." Both Ciapusci and Zeni are still tended by the original families, and DuPratt has been producing world class Zinfandel since it was planted, in 1916. Part of Ciapusci's original winery is still standing, there are tunnels in the mountain, used for wine storage, at Zeni, and parts of an old wine press can be found at DuPratt.

## First wines

Greenwood Ridge Vineyards had the honor of releasing the first wines bearing the Mendocino Ridge appellation. They included the 1996 Merlot, the 1997 White Riesling, and the 1997 Late Harvest White Riesling.

The Merlot is one of those wines that combines bright berry fruitiness, a long, soft, supple finish, and plenty of crisply

defined flavors, from cassis and black currant to the sharp spice of black pepper, all artfully balanced to make a complete package. The Rieslings, as usual, combine the almost "sweet-sour" contrast of apricot fruit (the sweet) and that razor-sharp steely, flinty, German "racy" quality (the sour) that virtually defines the finest of the varietal. The Late Harvest simply (though it's not really "simple" in any sense of the word) layers in the honey of *botrytis* and the thick, syrupy texture that comes with the enhanced (by severe dehydration) intensity of fruit, acid and texture that comes with the territory. Apricot is the focus of the late harvest fruit, but there are peach and pineapple notes tucked in if you look for them.

## Big growth on the horizon?

In a bold stroke, in the spring of 1999 Coastal Forestlands (a Mendocino County company) announced plans to plant up to 10,000 acres to vineyard within the Mendocino Ridge appellation and its immediate extension into Sonoma County at the southeastern corner of the new appellation (between Skaggs Springs Road [Sonoma County] and Mountain View Road [Mendocino County]). A winery would also be built, probably near Highway 101, near Cloverdale. "This will probably remain the largest vineyard planting project in Northern California for years to come if they are successful," the project consultant was quoted as saying.

While intended to be accomplished over a decade or two, the planting would indeed be a monumental addition to North Coast plantings. Sonoma County boasts some 45,000 acres and Mendocino has a mere 15,000 acres planted to the vine. To put this in perspective, the largest vineland holder in Sonoma County, Kendall-Jackson, has barely 4000 acres of vineyard.

A spokesman for Coastal Forestlands, in justification for a planting on so grand a scale, said simply, "The best grapes in the world can be produced in this area." He's right. (It should be well worth noting that all accounts indicate a large commitment by Coastal Forestlands—written into their planning process—to preserve wildlife habitat and indigenous woodlands with a conservation easement.)

"Coastal's environmental consultant says that they have plenty

*Most of the Mendocino Ridge region will remain just as you see it here, as few sites are suitable for the planting of wine grapes.*

of land that isn't good for growing trees, and that that's where they'll plant vines," says Allan Green. "If they do a good job of it, I'm all for it. One of the reasons that people are immediately horrified is that the company doesn't have a great reputation in their logging practices, so people see this as the next step for land that they've trashed in the past. So there are some major concerns to be addressed. But a well-planned, well-executed project, with proper environmental protections and mitigations, could be an example for the future."

Others are less sanguine. One farmer suggested that there are less than 500 additional acres that could reasonably be planted to the vine along the ridge. Another says that the accessible ridgetop locations are such that they could only support "two rows of vines, each a couple of miles long!"

47

What is proven is that, as Green says, "The coastal ridgetops do have great vineyard potential. The main concern is the political-social allegiances that are implied. Some will automatically put grape growers in with the loggers in the 'loggers versus environmentalists.' It really doesn't work that way."

All we know for sure is that the Mendocino Ridge is a special place for growing grapes, grapes that are the heart of some pretty interesting, decidedly distinctive wines. Of that much we are certain.

48

# White Wine on the Ridge

If Allan does not take himself seriously, at times, he always puts heart and soul into his wines. As cellarman Ronnie Karish notes, Allan has taken Fred Scherrer's Teutonic, no-nonsense approach to heart. "Fred was Mr. Detail," says Ronnie. "At a winery this small, it might be easy to let things slide occasionally, cut a corner when you're faced with a whole slew of tasks that need doing *right now*. But Fred sweated the details with the same intensity that would be expected at a much larger winery. Allan took that attitude to heart, and our wines have the benefit of it."

The approach is really no different than at any great winery: allow the grape to express the place it came from. When you ask Allan about picking decisions, his answer is by rote: "We want 24." On the surface, he's talking sugar. But the sub-text is only slightly more complicated. What he's saying is—again,

this is what all great winemakers are after—We want the fruit practically falling off the vine in the throes of maturity. We want every last ounce of flavor the bugger can give up. We want the essence of that grape variety, grown on that soil, in that particular climatic situation. We want, in short, identity. Individuality. Personality.

That's a big word, personality. How many human beings go the extra mile to develop and express an identity that stands out from the crowd? How few wines are capable of such expression. You'll meet more than a few here, because the folks at Greenwood Ridge Vineyards are finding, on a regular basis, wines that offer forth singular expression of individuality and identity. Which is what makes the whole exercise of winemaking worth doing. The challenge is clear, the results compelling.

## White Riesling: The White Knight

White Riesling appeals to our idealism, our love of innocence. White Riesling is the White Knight of varietal purity, where grape is translated into wine with the least loss of identity, with the most minimal diminution of resonance, intensity and singularity.

*Some White Rieslings nearly match the copper color of Greenwood Ridge Vineyard's capsule, generally ranging from straw-yellow to honey-gold in hue.*

Despite such individuality, despite being considered one of winedom's four "noble" varieties (along with Pinot Noir, Cabernet Sauvignon and Chardonnay), despite Riesling's low alcohol, despite its "racy," refreshing presence on the palate, Riesling is a variety in jeopardy. Catalogs do not list it, wine shops do not carry it, consumers do not buy it. 'Tis a puzzlement.

The source of Riesling's pure, innocent beauty has to do with fruit maturity (as distinguished from ripeness). Fruit maturity has to do with slow flavor development, usually in a climate that is, at best, barely warm enough to achieve that maturity on or near the last day of the available growing season.

Ripeness, on the other hand, is mere sugar development via sunshine and heat, or even dehydration. If you've ever tasted an apricot grown in too warm a location, you know the mealy, chewy, flavorless, cardboard-textured character it presents. If, on the other hand, you've tasted apricots grown in just the right microclimate, you know the juicy, fleshy, fresh, intense flavors that cascade about the tongue and dance upon the palate. That's flavor maturity. ("Maybe it's no coincidence that I grew up in an apricot orchard!" says Green with a hearty laugh.)

It is that juicy, bright, flavor-mature apricot that informs White Riesling grown in the right climate, from the cold northern climes of the Rhein or the Mosel to the Pacific-cooled slopes of Greenwood Ridge. It takes a decidedly cool place to grow flavorful Riesling.

Most of California fails on that account, and that is why Golden State-grown White Riesling has so little currency these days. But there are a few places, and this forested ridgeline is one of them. You can taste it in the current wines easily enough, but where it really shines is in the older wines, where great balance translates into a longevity that surprises and titillates. The 1989, fully a decade old as this book is written, remains vibrant, with tangy lime, apricot and honey notes. Even the 1983, all of sixteen seasons old as we are tasting it, is alive and lovely, with light apricot and orange peel fruit, and a flint-and-steel-infused, fusel oil texture that wraps around your tongue in a

*White Riesling grapes nearing perfect maturity:  pale green, speckled with brown, loaded with succulent, sweet juice, and coated with morning dew.*

silky, slinky fashion.  Bring on the tarragon-laced halibut, this wine's ready.  Astonishingly, the very first Greenwood Ridge Vineyards Riesling, the 1980, still shows youthful color (straw yellow), fruit vibrancy (flinty apricot) and beautifully aged texture (fusel oil and glycerol).  Still crisp and clean at nearly two decades of age.

Young, the Greenwood Ridge White Riesling shows the apricot readily, with a tropical sidebar that features pineapple and mango notes that only add to the often honied richness and complexity of a varietal not normally known for depth and complexity.  But it's there, bolstered neatly by that stone-like, incisive "raciness" the Germans so love to talk about, that zingy textural quality that pushes the fruit forward and lays the groundwork for ageability.  Tangy is a good descriptor, but isn't quite sufficient standing alone.  You have to taste the wines to get the full effect.

"We haven't really changed anything with the Riesling since we starting making it in 1980," says Allan.  "We've always aimed at off-dry, with a residual sugar of about one point five: tart enough to give you that pleasing sweet-and-sour tang that goes so well with spicy foods, yet rich enough to stand alone as a sipping wine."

Allan also sees his Riesling as something of a "novice" wine, a wine suited to those without an extensive wine background who might be put off by the wholly dry Chardonnay or Sauvignon Blanc, folks who would gravitate toward a White Zinfandel at some other winery.

"We thought about making Gewürztraminer," he says with a smile, "but there are already so many fine ones made around here—Navarro, Lazy Creek, Handley, Husch, Edmeades—that we figured we'd stay with our own niche."

The four acres of Riesling are usually hand-harvested into half-ton plastic bins the first week of October.  "If we have a crew of twenty—and the old block and the new block both ripen at the same time (or it looks like it's going to rain for a week!)—we can pick all the Riesling in a single day," Allan says.  "That's a lot faster than we can process the fruit in the winery, so when that happens we have to crush and press well into the night.  At least the nights are cool that time of year, so it's not going to hurt the fruit or the juice.  But things rarely work out that perfectly, anyway."

Under normal conditions, fruit for the regular (relatively non-botrytised) Riesling is picked at about 23 degrees Brix.  The fruit is crushed, pressed, allowed to settle for two days, then racked.  "Between a fairly cold fermentation—at 57 degrees Fahrenheit—and the use of Epernay yeast, we are able to maintain the floral aromatics that come with the fruit," says Allan.  "The Epernay yeast is not a particularly strong yeast, which is a help to us when we're trying to stop the fermentation at about one-and-a-half percent residual sugar.  The fermentation might be impossible to stop with another, stronger yeast strain."

When the fermentation begins to slow near the end, it is occasionally necessary to let it warm up five to eight degrees—simply by turning the chiller off—to burn off those last few degrees of sugar.  The fermentation typically takes about three weeks, but can last up to two or three months.  The wine is bottled when the portable bottling line makes its April run up to the ridge.

# Chardonnay

Chardonnay in California is a true conundrum. For the most part, the variety has been planted in warmish climes—the intention being to get the fruit off the vine well before the rains threaten (a timid, safety factor wholly unrelated to fruit/wine quality concerns)—so that the resulting wines tend to be overripe and heavily alcoholic, wines so out-sized that they are usually "enhanced" by layers of roasty-toasty oak. As if this were a good thing (or, more likely, might divert one's attention from the unbalanced base wine).

Green got into producing Chardonnay rather by accident. "I had met John Schultz when I spoke at a U.C. Davis winemaking seminar around 1985," Allan recalls. "He was from Utah, and his dream and ambition was to move to Anderson Valley, grow grapes and make wine. But he figured it would be smart to establish his brand—have some wines produced for his label—before he moved here, so he asked me to make some Chardonnay for him.

"Hey, I was flattered. Plus, I figured I could practice on someone else's Chardonnay. Fred was here at that time. We bought some Chardonnay fruit from Ulysses Lolonis, over in Redwood Valley, and made a couple of vintages for John in 1986 and

*Ronnie Karish adds rice hulls as he fills the press with Chardonnay must. The rice hulls facilitate increased juice yields at lower pressures.*

1987. By 1988, he came to the realization that his timetable was decelerating, that he wasn't going to be moving here soon, and that there was no advantage to continue."

So, Green bought Schultz's 1988 vintage for his own label, began buying DuPratt Vineyard fruit in 1990 (blending the two vineyards for two years), then sticking solely with DuPratt fruit from the 1992 vintage onward. That has been a good choice, for the DuPratt Vineyard—Green's nearest Mendocino Ridge neighbor—grows absolutely sumptuous Chardonnay fruit. Tom and Michelle Krig, a couple of Los Angelinos who have owned DuPratt Vineyard since 1989, deliver Chardonnay that is fairly bursting with sweet apple and lemon, has a firm, mineral spine that holds the fruit together, and takes a smattering of French oak that adds a subtle hint of graham to a lush and lengthy cream texture.

Grown in a relatively cool climate, Chardonnay here achieves a lean, almost sinewy mineral backbone that holds the fruit in close. What that means is that you have a structure built for aging. The wine doesn't fall apart from a lack of internal inertia. It is, in essence, a non-California structure (flabby, too much alcohol, too much oak, little or no fruit), and that is to the good. Taste the 1994 Chardonnay, if you can find some. It is still bright and vibrant, with fleshy apricot, pear, peach, lime and honeysuckle fruit. As important, the wine is beginning to richen out in the mouth, with an oily, richly viscous texture that is alluringly supple. This is what Chardonnay is supposed to be in California . . . if it is planted in the right place. That's a mighty big *if*.

"We try to get the fruit at about 24 degrees Brix," says Allan as if this were news. "Mainly we rely on their vineyard manager, Steve Tylicki, who is also our vineyard consultant, to be out there tasting the fruit. He's very experienced and talented at tasting grapes. He's able to taste the fruit and determine where it's going to go from there. When it will be fully mature, in terms of flavor. That's the key."

Green notes that malolactic fermentation is essential to Char-

donnay grown in this cool a climate, otherwise the resulting wine would go over the opposite edge, into acidity so razor sharp that it would be a caricature of austerity. "We usually pick the Chardonnay in mid-October, and 24 sugar will give us around fourteen percent alcohol, but the wine is in such balance that you don't notice it.

"We crush and press into stainless steel tanks, let the juice settle for a few days, then add yeast and rack into barrels for both primary and malolactic fermentations. We initially tried Epernay 2 yeast, but it's not a strong finisher, and we can't afford stuck fermentations. So we switched to Prise de Mousse, which is a sure-fire finisher. We complete our fermentation in barrel in about ten days, then leave the wine on the lees—stirring about every three weeks—until May or June, and bottle it in July or August.

"It's all the time on the lees that really gives the wine that creamy texture that you talk about. Only about twenty percent, perhaps a little more, goes into new oak. We want the fruit to show itself. That's what's supposed to define a wine, isn't it? The fruit? We think so."

Partly due to the strong demand for Greenwood Ridge's other wines, and partly due to the fact that there are only a million Chardonnays on the market today, the winery has cut Chardonnay production from about 700 cases a year down to 400. But the wine is too good to phase out entirely. Taste it, and you'll have a new understanding of what California Chardonnay can, and should, be.

## Sauvignon Blanc

Sadly, Sauvignon Blanc does not yet have the cachet of Chardonnay in California. Perhaps one day it will, because it is certainly better suited to be grown throughout most of California's winegrowing climes, which tend towards the warm side of the spectrum.

Like Chardonnay, at Greenwood Ridge Vineyards, Sauvignon

Blanc's presence on the wine list is near to happenstance. "When we opened the tasting room, in 1986, I realized that we didn't have a dry white wine to pour," confesses Green almost sheepishly. "We began getting our Sauvignon Blanc from Ferrington Vineyard, just this side of Boonville, behind Roederer's vineyard on the north side of Highway 128. It's significantly warmer there than it is here in the western end of the valley.

*It only takes a couple of candles and a bottle of wine, like the Sauvignon Blanc below, to create a romantic mood.*

"We get a portion of our Sauvignon Blanc from Elizabeth Vineyards, over in Redwood Valley. We had made some wine for her label, and really liked its quality. A couple of years ago, starting in 1997, we also began getting Sauvignon Blanc and some Semillon from Bill and Gail Meyer, whose small vineyard is further up the hill, behind Ferrington."

Semillon adds a fleshy, almost "fat" quality to Sauvignon Blanc which, on its own, tends to be more severe, a bit sharper, and often possesses a slight but necessary bitterness in the finish. "We're not afraid to slip in a percent or two of Riesling to tone the bitterness down to manageable levels if it's too pronounced," announces Green, "and we'll blend in a touch of Chardonnay to round things out in years when the Sauvignon Blanc is on the thin side, structurally. Sometimes it's just to soften the varietal's natural grassiness, when that gets a bit out of hand. We want balance. We want the best possible wine. It's what ends up in the glass, after all, that matters most."

Though Sauvignon Blanc doesn't have a particularly high profile in most wine circles, Greenwood Ridge's 1989 earned "Best White Wine" at the 1990 West Coast Wine Competition in Reno. Understandable given that the wine shows a mineral-steely, firm bell pepper and freshly-mowed grass varietal character, shaded with a lemon-herbal-melon fleshiness that expands in the mouth fluidly, with the occasional peach note as accent.

"We want that varietal balance between the grass and the melon," says Green. "A little of each, but not too much of one over the other. We always talk about balance, and it probably gets a little old after a time, but that's what makes it work. If you have balance, everything else falls into place. Now that we have access to some Semillon, from the Meyer's place, we probably won't need to do any other blending to achieve the balance we're after. Semillon's kind of amazing, in that it can taste really mature at fairly low sugar levels."

Elizabeth Vineyards is usually picked first (it's in a warmer location), followed by the Ferrington fruit. Those two lots,

usually the first into the winery, are barrel fermented, while the Meyer lot, which usually comes in last, is fermented in stainless. "It's really a matter of availability," notes Green. "It depends on how much space we have in tanks or in barrels at the time the fruit is mature. It's all one big juggling act at that time of year. You can feel like you're part of a circus."

Picked from late September through mid-October, the wines remain in barrel until they are bottled in April. Only a very small portion of the oak is new, usually about ten percent. Most goes into once-used Chardonnay barrels.

How long between bottling and release? "Twenty-four hours!" jokes Allan. "Don't laugh. We've done that. Four months would be nice, but the wine doesn't really need it. It's ready to go once it hits the bottle. So, if we're sold out, and the restaurants are clamoring for it, it's there for them. You always hate to run out of any given wine, because you don't want to give up that shelf slot in the store, that position on the wine list in the restaurant. If you manage your allocations just right, you run out just when the next vintage is ready. But if you win a big award, the wine just blows out the door, and you're stuck between a rock and a hard place.

"But there's not as much influence from the medals these days. Perhaps it's because people are finally starting to trust their own palates. I hope so. Probably it's more that magazines are so busy promoting their own tasting panels that they don't give as much space or attention to the wine judgings and their awards, medals, prizes. So I suppose it's up to the wineries to get the word out . . . if they're not too busy making wine!"

GREENWOOD RIDGE VINEYARDS

MENDOCINO RIDGE

MERLOT

1997

ESTATE BOTTLED

ALCOHOL 13.5% BY VOLUME

Located six miles from the ocean on a ridgetop overlooking Anderson Valley in Mendocino County, Greenwood Ridge Vineyards has produced limited amounts of hand crafted wine in small case lots since 1980.

A blend of 78% Merlot and 22% Cabernet Sauvignon, this wine was aged for 16 months in French oak barrels. Spicy herbal aromas blend with those of cherries and cassis in harmony with a bouquet of toasted oak. With rich yet elegant flavors of raspberry and chocolate that linger on the palate, this Merlot will complement the heartiest stews and red meats.

Grown, produced and bottled by
Greenwood Ridge Vineyards
Philo, California U.S.A. 707-895-2002

CONTAINS SULFITES

GOVERNMENT WARNING: (1) ACCORDING TO THE SURGEON GENERAL, WOMEN SHOULD NOT DRINK ALCOHOLIC BEVERAGES DURING PREGNANCY BECAUSE OF THE RISK OF BIRTH DEFECTS. (2) CONSUMPTION OF ALCOHOLIC BEVERAGES IMPAIRS YOUR ABILITY TO DRIVE A CAR OR OPERATE MACHINERY, AND MAY CAUSE HEALTH PROBLEMS.

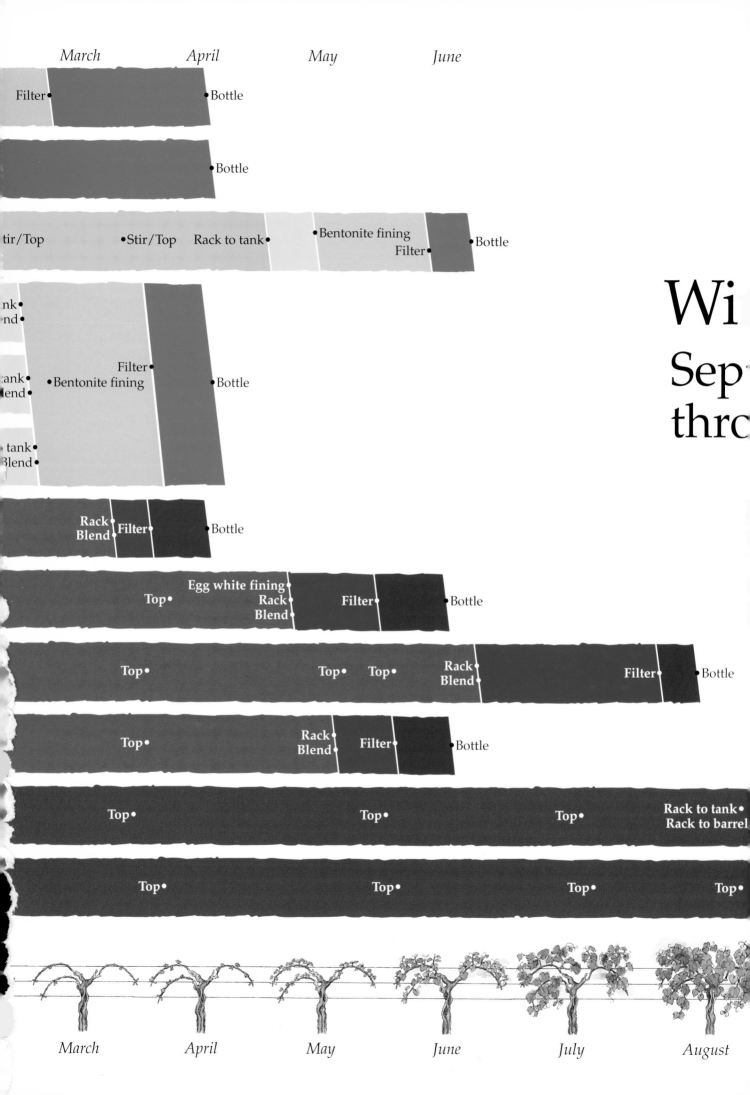

September 1997 | October | November | December | January 1998 | February

**'97 White Riesling**
- Crush/Press•
- Rack/Filter lees•
- Add yeast•
- Rack•
- Bentonite fining•

**'97 Late Harvest White Riesling**
- Crush/Press•
- Rack/Filter lees•
- Rack•
- Add yeast•
- Filter•

**'97 Chardonnay**
- Crush/Press•
- Rack/Filter lees•
- Add yeast••Rack to barrels
- •Consolidate barrels
- •Top
- •Stir/Top
- •Stir/Top
- •Stir/Top

**'97 Sauvignon Blanc** *(Elizabeth Vineyards)*
- Crush/Press•
- Rack/Filter lees•
- Add yeast••Rack to barrels
- •Consolidate barrels
- •Top
- •Top
- •Top
- Rack to B

**'97 Sauvignon Blanc** *(Yorkville Vineyards)*
- Crush/Press•
- Rack/Filter lees•
- Add yeast••Rack to barrels
- •Consolidate barrels
- •Top
- •Top
- •Top
- Rack to

**'97 Sauvignon Blanc** *(Meyer Vineyards)*
- Crush/Press•
- Rack/Filter lees•
- Add yeast•
- •Rack to barrels
- •Top
- •Top
- •Top
- Rack t

**'96 Merlot**
- Top•
- Top•
- Top•
- Top•

**'96 Cabernet Sauvignon**
- Top•
- Top•
- Top•
- Top•

**'97 Zinfandel**
- Crush•
- Add yeast•
- Press•
- Rack•
- •Rack to barrels
- Top•
- Top•
- Top•
- Top•

**'97 Pinot Noir**
- Crush•
- Add yeast•
- Press•
- Rack•
- •Rack to barrels
- Top•
- •Top
- Top•
- Top•

**'97 Merlot**
- Crush•
- Add yeast•
- Press
- •Rack
- Rack to barrels•
- Top•
- Top•
- Top•

**'97 Cabernet Sauvignon**
- Crush•
- Add yeast•
- Press
- •Rack to barrels
- Top•
- Top•
- To

September 1997 | October | November | December | January 1998 | February

# Annual Vineyard Timeline

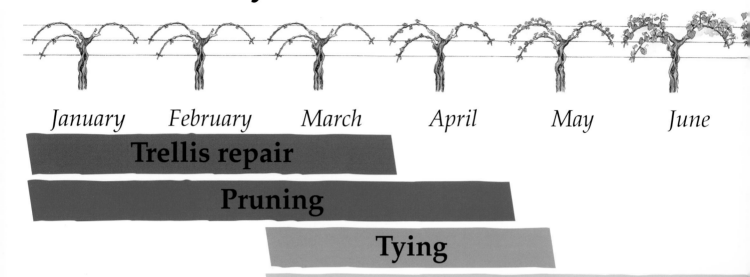

| January | February | March | April | May | June |
|---------|----------|-------|-------|-----|------|

**Trellis repair**

**Pruning**

**Tying**

**Weed control**

**Crown suckering**

**Trunk suckering**

**Mildew con**

**Replanting**

**Petiole**

*Bud break*

*Blo*

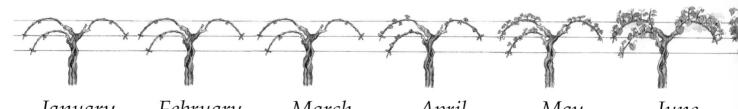

| January | February | March | April | May | June |
|---------|----------|-------|-------|-----|------|

tr...

Prebottling

sampl...

Lea... ...bottling

...om

Blend
Rack

Filter • Bottle

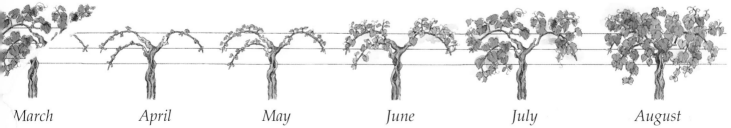

March          April          May          June          July          August

# making Timeline

nber 1997
h August 1999

| White Wine | | | | |
|---|---|---|---|---|
| | Settling | Fermentation | Malolatic fermentation | Ageing |

st

| Red Wine | | | | |
|---|---|---|---|---|
| | Fermentation & punch down | Settling | Malolatic fermentation | Ageing |

Top•  '97 Merlot  Top•  Egg white fining•  Top•
Top•

ck to tank  Top•  '97 Cabernet  Top•  Egg white fining•
ack to barrels  Sauvignon  Top•

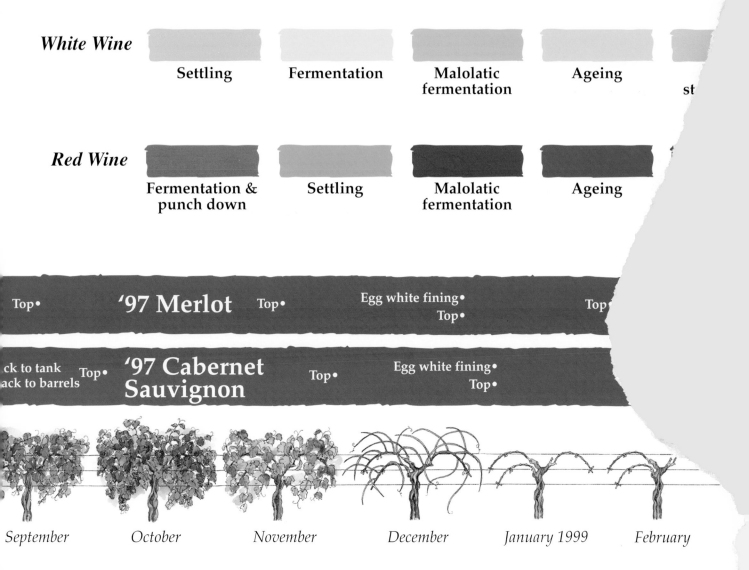

September          October          November          December          January 1999          February

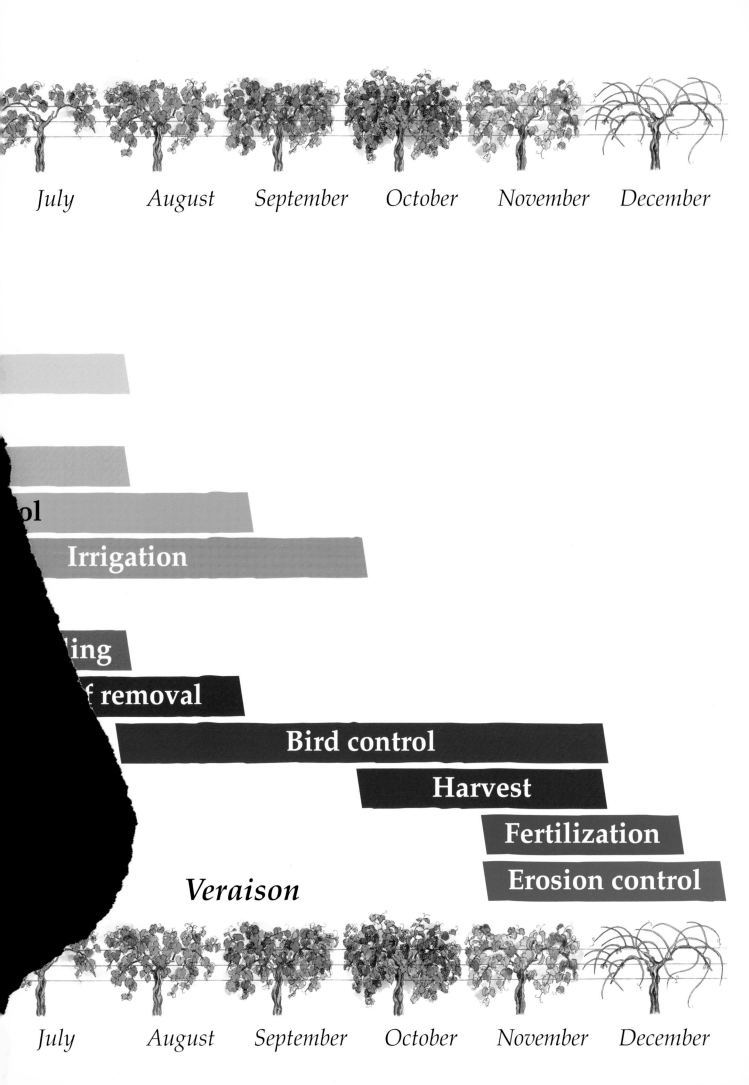

July     August     September     October     November     December

ol

**Irrigation**

ling

f removal

**Bird control**

**Harvest**

**Fertilization**

**Erosion control**

*Veraison*

July     August     September     October     November     December

In case you're wondering who does all the work depicted on these timelines: Ron Karish (above), Efrain Ramirez (top right) and Samuel Barragan (lower right) all have been with Greenwood Ridge Vineyards for many years. Not pictured is their colleague, the bashful Pedro Viramontes.

# Red Wine...and Dessert

## Pinot Noir

This is the reason we're all here, class. This is the reason wines are made, here or anywhere else in the world. Great Pinot Noir is the justification for all of it.

Let me explain. Pinot Noir, when grown in the right place and made with great and painstaking attention to detail, is about sensuality. When it is done well, Pinot Noir is so supple, so fleshy, so juicy, so "wet," so utterly and downright decadent that it inspires one to create new sins . . . and wish to commit them! (Write that down, if you must, and get the attribution correct. It's called "Hinkle's Second Wine Law.")

As you might expect, by now, Pinot Noir was not added to the Greenwood Ridge Vineyards list out of sensual or *sinsual* inspiration. No, it was just another copacetic, accidental bit of good luck. Allan's new winemaker simply wanted to make

*Harvest is always a time of great energy and enthusiasm. Especially the first harvest of Greenwood Ridge Vineyard's estate Pinot Noir grapes, in October of 1999, which had been eagerly anticipated since the grapes were planted in 1996.*

some.

"Yeah, that's about it," shrugs Green in mock defiant resignation. "Van Williamson had just come aboard, and he really wanted to make Pinot Noir. I mean, he was *really* excited about the possibilities of Pinot Noir up here. So I said, 'If we can get some good grapes, sure. Why not?'"

Real focused, this guy. But, hey, some of the greatest artistic creations are serendipitous from the outset. So, in Allan Green's immortal words, "Why not?"

"We got all the fruit for our first vintage, 1989, from Roederer Estate," says Allan. "They had extra fruit in those days, and were happy to help us out. The following year we also had some fruit from Christine Woods, a vineyard and winery near

Handley Cellars. But ever since then, the largest part of the fruit has always been from the Roederer Estate."

Roederer is, of course, the superb sparkling wine producer (owned by the venerable French Champagne house of the same name) just down the highway from the Greenwood Ridge Vineyards tasting room. "Michel Salgues, their winemaster, has always been gracious enough to set aside a tiny portion of their vineyard to hang long after the rest of their vines have been harvested for sparkling wine. Over the years, the success of their wines has made it increasingly difficult for Michel to hold back some for us, so we finally planted four acres of Pinot here at the winery in 1996. We had developed something of a following and, hey, I like Pinot Noir too. Michel's been good enough to save a little for us each year until our own vines are fully into production in the year 2000. We've never had a contract. We just sort of discuss it as we go. I trust him, he trusts me."

That cooperative aspect of the wine business has always been one of its finest assets. There is not a winemaker alive in California who cannot regale you with stories of intra-winery generosity for hours on end. "Oh, sure," says Allan with a broad grin. "That happens all the time, especially around here

*Half-ton bins receive buckets of grapes, hand-harvested by practiced picking crews.*

*It takes great skill to wield a picker's knife without taking a knuckle or two with a cluster of Pinot Noir.*

where we're all small and all far removed from the main corridors of commerce. One year, our Merlot was late, our Cabernet was falling off the vine, and we desperately needed some extra fermenting tanks. I got on the phone, and ended up borrowing one milk tank each from Handley, Husch and Obester [now Goldeneye, owned by Napa Valley's Duckhorn Vineyard]. A few bottles of wine changed hands, and no one felt out of sorts.

"One year, our portable bottler ran out of glue, and it only took a few phone calls to find someone who had some that would work with their equipment. Before we had a lees filter—that's a good chunk of cash for a small winery—we'd drive our lees down to Handley Cellars and use theirs when they weren't using it. Here in Anderson Valley, we all borrow and we all loan. Although we're not usually the first to be called, up here on the hill, we're always happy to pour other wineries' wines for them at the various tasting events we all attend."

Pinot Noir does represent a slight diversion for Green, but no more so than some of the other wines he's chosen (or *been* chosen) to make. He'll admit to a slight case of schizophrenia in the matter. "We are up here on this high ridge, and that does separate us from the Anderson Valley proper," he explains tactfully. "We aren't like the rest of Anderson Valley. We make Merlot and Cabernet Sauvignon. They're known for Pinot Noir, Gewürztraminer and Chardonnay.

"Okay, we make a little Chardonnay. Yeah, I know. I've spent

*The winery hires only 49er fans during harvest, which of course occurs in the middle of football season.*

twenty years promoting Anderson Valley, and I'm still a part of the group in every way but climate. It's the camaraderie that really counts. That's what holds us all together up here. That and the commonly held ideal of creating great wines."

It will be interesting to see how the ridgeline vineyard Pinot Noir shows itself. What's been made thus far does indeed inspire innocently impure thoughts, with its supple, very soft black cherry and plum fruitiness, sometimes jammy, spiced with tangy cola notes, and framed by toasted French oak that occasionally reminds of black walnut meat. The 1996 is a particular favorite of mine, with its hothouse nutmeg and brown sugar spiciness and fleshy, ripe black cherry and tomato notes that simply dance on the tongue and linger on the palate. (This wine won "Best New World Pinot Noir" at the 1998 New World International Wine Competition.)

The 1997 is an instructive wine. "It was beautiful when it first came out, with lots of black cherry fruit, but then it went into kind of a funk," assesses Allan. My first tasting, in November of 1998, showed a thorn-sharp, combative wine, with ligneous, green tomato fruit. Wholly unlike any of the others. By May of '99 the wine was beginning to come around again, the black cherry back in front, with earthy, almost leathery ripe tomato and lovely hints of mushroom in the middle and in the finish. These mood swings are not entirely unusual for the Pinot. Beaulieu's gnomic legend, Andre Tchelistcheff, once told me that he was ready to toss the best Pinot he ever made—the 1946—down the drain at at least three stages . . . before it even made it to bottle. "And it went through a few blue periods even in bottle," laughed the Russian leprechaun, his bushy eyebrows dancing with hilarity.

The Greenwood Ridge Vineyards Pinot Noir is usually picked in mid-October. "We do taste the fruit, but Michel makes the decision on when to pick," admits Allan. "Michel will call and say, 'I think we're going to pick your grapes tomorrow.' We've never been disappointed with any of his decisions. They pick into 800-pound French fruit bins and we handle it like all of our reds: we de-stem, the juice goes into stainless steel milk tanks, and we inoculate with Pasteur Red or L2226 yeast.

"We punch the cap down three or four times a day with a twelve-inch teflon square attached to a shovel handle. We press the juice off the skins when it still has a little sugar left and start the malolactic at that time, while the juice is still a little warm. We don't want to lose the ML bugs in the pomace, and we don't want to artificially warm up the juice just to induce the malolactic fermentation.

"Since all of our wines—except the Riesling—go into barrel, we've got a lot of barrels [more than 300] for a small winery." Green buys nearly a hundred new barrels every year, selling off used barrels wholesale for $15 apiece to friends at an Albion nursery, who sell them for planters. A rather ignominious ending for a (new) $600 work of art.

Green uses barrels from two coopers (Dargaud & Jaegle and Francois Freres) and wood from five different French forests (Nevers, Trocais, Allier, Vosges and Bertranges). "I'm really not that experimental. This works, so we keep it that way. I like the complexity that we get from a blend of several forests. We have done several tastings, and this blend always seems to do the best. We don't use Limousin oak. I've never liked the taste of those barrels.

"Our Pinot Noir gets about eight months in oak, about thirty-five to forty percent new oak, and is bottled in August. We try to get six months in bottle prior to release, typically. Of course we do send it out to our Advance Tasting Club members prior to its release."

## Zinfandel

If you're going to guess that this idiosyncratic variety's arrival at Greenwood Ridge was equally happenstance, you'll be right, as usual. "This is the irony of ironies," says Green with a tilt of his head. "We spend so much of our time focusing on local products, promoting Anderson Valley and now Mendocino Ridge, it's a wry fact that the wine that really put us on the map, the one wine that has consistently won more medals at more competitions than almost any other in the state—including two "Best of Shows"—is the only non-Mendocino County wine that we make!"

He is referring, of course, to the fluid, fruit-packed, seriously juicy Scherrer Vineyards Zinfandel. "It was a winemaker thing, naturally," Allan says with a self-deprecating grin. "Fred Scherrer had come to work for us in 1985, so it just seemed natural that we'd make a little wine from his family's vineyard. It's in the Alexander Valley, up there on the bench behind Sausal Winery. You *know* that's good ground for Zinfandel. We got two loads back in 1986, maybe four tons. Sent the truck down there. Even after Fred left to go to Dehlinger Winery [he's now working on his own label], we continued getting grapes from his dad, Edwin."

Allan whistles when he describes the vineyard. "Oh, it's just the most carefully taken-care-of vineyard you've ever seen! Everything is so *even*. You go through the rows after the leaves have been pulled, and it looks like the vines are standing at attention for a military inspection, everything is so precise, so perfect. Edwin, Fred, and Fred's sister Louise, really know what they're doing. The family's been growing grapes there since 1912."

The Scherrers know that Allan wants the fruit falling-off-the-vine ripe. As with Roederer, there is no contract. "We've been getting the fruit from them for fourteen years now, and never a problem," says Green. "Of course I make very sure to pay the bill very quickly!" The winery normally gets 12 to 15 tons of fruit. "These are very old vines, but the part we get is trained on cordons. The grapes are all in a perfect line [spreading his arms out wide], all the leaves pulled, all the fruit out in the sun, looking like a machine had done it, everything is so exact."

In a normal year, Pasteur Red yeast is employed, but if it looks like the alcohols are going to be above 14%, L2226 will be used, as it's a bit more alcohol tolerant. Nearly three-quarters of the barrels used for the Zinfandel are water-bent American oak. "We're trying some barrels made from oak grown in Oregon. It has a strong toasty character to it. We'll see how it does."

In 1996 a second Zinfandel was produced, from Elizabeth Vineyards in Redwood Valley. "It was good Zinfandel, but it proved too confusing to our customers to have two Zins. It worked as wine, but not as a marketing idea."

The Scherrer Zinfandel has been universally recognized as exceptional, and it will only take a taste or two to prove it. The wine exhibits an extraordinary juiciness for having so much and so intense a fruit definition, which typically includes cranberry, cherry, chocolate, plum, raspberry and strawberry. Most Zinfandels, with that much fruit power, finish dry and dusty. No chance of that here. Check out the '95 if you can find it. The bright cranberry and cherry really spread out in

the mouth, with a light sprinkling of peppercorn spice that brightens up the already zingy fruit. The weight, or mouth-feel, is light to medium, yet there is so much fruit there that you'd tend to call the wine big. Maybe Muhammad Ali's "Float like a butterfly, sting like a bee" comes closest to describing this apparent contradiction of size and weight perception. Even when the alcohols are high and the fruit expression jammy, the texture remains silky, fluid and juicy. Impressive.

The 1997 is showing pretty well, too. Southern California retailer Randy Kemner, in his newsletter *The Wine Country*, writes of one taster lauding the wine's balance. "I agreed, even though the rich, briary, cedary, buttery, ripe berry flavors were rich and full and captured my attention first. The very next day I got on the phone and ordered five more cases of this wonderful wine."

# Merlot

Tony and Gretchen Husch had planted 2.5 acres of Merlot in 1972 (along with nearly equal amounts of Cabernet Sauvignon and White Riesling), little knowing that it would prove out as possibly *the* variety best suited to this ridgetop location, barely six miles from the Pacific.

Taste through the wines. Even the older vintages continue to show plush plum, menthol and tobacco fruit, with hints of green olive, that define the softest of the Bordeaux varieties (when grown in the right place).

Until Louis Martini and Ric Forman (at Sterling Vineyards) began to produce Merlot as a varietal wine, this understated-but-enriching charmer had been passed off as mere blending material for Cabernet Sauvignon, Lou Costello's lesser, comedic foil to the stronger, more serious lead of Bud Abbott. But if you've ever tasted the soft-but-long St. Emilions (the best—Ausone, Canon, Pavie—are on high limestone terraces or hilltops) or the richer Pomerols (Petrus is also on a hilltop), you know what subtle character derives from this essentially modest little red grape.

"Merlot grows differently than other grape varieties," muses

*Mature Merlot fruit falling from the picking bin into the receiving hopper, from which the fruit will be augered into the de-stemmer, which removes the berries from the stems.*

Green. "Its shoots like to grow *down*. Our vines were originally trained vertically, but when that didn't work too well, we tried several different methods, finally settling on a Geneva Double Curtain [GDC]. With the GDC, we can take advantage of that tendency, and make it work for us. When the canes begin to flop over, we let 'em flop down, which really opens up the canopy to sunlight . . . without our having to do a lot of canopy management: leaf stripping and the like. The GDC is the ideal means for getting the canes out of the middle of the vine, where they want to go, and out of the way so that the fruit is more exposed. It's almost like having two rows in one, but with the ability to get great quality at more than five tons per acre."

Another thing Allan discovered is that Merlot will set and try to mature an awful lot of fruit if left to its own devices. "We definitely have to do a little thinning every year. We got eleven tons per acre in 1994, and that was way too much. The trick is to balance yields from year to year, so you don't get that yo-yo effect, suffering mightily in the years after great abundance."

The fruit usually matures in late October, with 24 sugar—where have we heard that before?—as the goal. After that, it's pretty straightforward winemaking. Only the barreling is a slight exception, using the thin stave, Bordeaux "Chateau" barrels. "We use only Nevers oak for Merlot and Cabernet," says Allan, "coopered by Nadalie. We get half our barrels at 'medium toast' and half at 'medium-plus' toast, whatever that means. We just like what those toasting levels add, as a subtle spice, to the wine. We never want the oak to impinge on the fruit. We usually bottle our Merlot in April of the following year, so it gets about fifteen months in oak. The Cabernet doesn't get bottled until June, so it gets about eighteen months in oak."

The 1996 Merlot—the first red wine to bear the new "Mendocino Ridge" appellation—is a stunning bottle of red wine. The fruit is exquisitely defined, with cassis, red currant and bright berry, with a light black pepper spice shaded by the graham of French oak in just the right proportion. Given all the fruit focus and fair size and weight, the wine remains supple and fluid in the mouth, and the fruit hangs there on the palate for several minutes after the last swallow. Not bad for a grape that was, for the longest time, considered Cabernet's lesser sidekick.

## Cabernet Sauvignon

This is the real revelation here, for Anderson Valley was long considered far too cold a clime to get any real flavor maturity out of this stubborn, late ripening variety. Yes, Allan does have the advantage of being up on a ridgetop, out of the fog, basking in the sunshine on one of those vinous islands we have talked about. But it remains a challenge to get King Red mature enough to expose itself fully and completely in the glass, and in some years—like 1993, when the wine was sold off in bulk, it was so unripe—it is simply not possible at all. Same thing

happened in 1998. Cool season, fruit flavors never quite made it . . . out the back door.

"That's hard to do," admits Green with a crack in his voice. "But we know what it can be when the flavors are mature, and we can't proudly put our name on the label when they don't get there." That sounds simple and straightforward. And on one level it is. It's still a tough decision to have to make. But make it you must.

That said, when it works, it works wondrously. Like the '92— a wine still mouth-filling with ripe cassis, sweet tobacco, anise, green bean and cherry—which won "Best of Show" at the Los Angeles County Fair a couple of years later. Like the 1995, which is showing best now, flush with tobacco, menthol, black currant and lusciously ripe blackberry fruit, accented with cedar and graham oak spiciness that serves only to push the

*Cabernet Sauvignon "must" (juice and berries, fresh from the de-stemmer) is pumped into a stainless steel fermenting tank.*

fruit further into the foreground.  This is a wine whose abundant fruit and satin texture simply spread out in the mouth in grand profusion.  Set a glass next to a rare filet mignon, slathered with mushrooms, and Heaven is just around the corner.

Getting to that point does take a bit of effort.  In the vineyard it means constant attention to extensive leaf-pulling and the re-positioning of canes so that fruit clusters are not shaded.  "It's really saying 'To hell with sunburn,'" says Green matter-of-factly.  "If they get it, they get it.  Exposing the grapes to the sun is of the utmost importance, because if we don't, there's no chance of reaching the fruit maturity we need, the flavor development that is essential to producing a memorable wine.  It's taken awhile to get to that point, to learn that lesson and *trust* it enough to actually take the necessary loss of sunburnt fruit.  But that's the price you pay.  When the results are this good, it's worth the price."

*Cabernet "must" begins its fermentation, the transformation of sugar into carbon dioxide and ethanol, by means of yeast.*

*A hydrometer (the glass stem floating in the grape juice) measures a sugar content of just over 25° Brix.*

The four acres of Cabernet, planted in 1972 (own roots) and 1975 (St. George rootstock), are trained on a three-wire trellis and cane-pruned. "We don't use catch wires, so the vines develop a bit of a sprawl," explains Green. "But Cabernet makes short canes—unlike Riesling—and the canes are strong. They don't break off in the wind, and we do get some pretty good afternoon breezes up here, exposed as we are. They stay up on their own, so fruit-shading isn't a huge problem. But we do have to watch for it, because any shading at all compromises our shot at full and complete flavor maturity."

In the winery, things are pretty straightforward, except that a lot of hand work is involved in bucketing the cap off all the reds. "We don't punch down the cap on the day before we press," says Allan. "By moving the cap to the press by hand, bucket by bucket, we lower the hard tannins significantly. This has brought a major improvement to our reds, but particularly to the Cabernet. Our old must pump just wasn't that gentle. By handling these cap solids so carefully, we get reds with much silkier textures and a distinctively more fluid mouth-feel. It really does make a world of difference."

Green notes that he used to try a little American oak in the aging process, but felt that that distinctive dill character couldn't be avoided. "When wine prices pushed up a bit, it got to where we could afford the French oak we needed for the Cabernet. But American oak barrels are so much better than they used to be, so it's not set in stone that we'll *never* use American oak for the Cabernet. We're also bringing the Cabernet price down a bit, to put it in line with our Pinot Noir, Merlot and Chardonnay. We were getting significant resistance from our Mendocino County distributor, who was saying 'The wine is plenty good, but we just can't sell Mendocino Cabernet at that price.' Dropping the price wasn't all that difficult for me to do. Hey, I never want to have a wine that would force people to say, 'This is good, but kind of expensive."

On the day Allan and I are tasting and talking about the Cabernet—basking in the spring sun on the tasting room deck— we discover that a casino host from Harrah's has driven down from Reno specifically to secure three cases of the '95 Cabernet for their Steakhouse Restaurant . . . to satisfy one of their high roller regulars. (The high roller, it turns out, runs a Bay Area investment firm and usually drinks Lafite and Latour. In a carefully timed aside, the host notes that the fellow's name happens to be remarkably similar to that of the winery. "But," enthusiastically assures the host, "he really likes your wine!")

## Late Harvest White Riesling

If you've got any kind of sweet tooth at all, here is the justification for its existence. Tasting and drinking this stuff is like the kid latching on to the key to the candy store, only now you're an adult and you can really appreciate something this sweet, something this sinuous, something this syrupy and sensual all at the same time.

I once wrote an article on botrytised beauties entitled *How to Spot an Alien*. The thesis of the article was simple enough: If you didn't like these luxuriously sweet lovelies . . . you had to be from another planet! Or solar system! It is nearly without any plausibility whatsoever that someone claiming *homo sapiens* status would not fall in love over these honied delights.

If you've ever had a problem understanding the word *cornucopia*, botrytised wines give you the opportunity to fully comprehend the word's insistence on thorough and complete abundance. For these are wines that open up the thesaurus on "sweet" and "syrupy" and "ample fruit."

Allan can tell you how the wines are made later. Let me tell you about the wines. Now. Apricot and honey are the usual early descriptors, because they are the essence of Riesling and botrytis, respectively. When the "noble mold" (*botrytis cinerea*) becomes established on Riesling berries, the berries dehydrate without breaking the skin. Thus, the natural fruit and acidity are magnified in intensity manyfold. What's there becomes focused, big time.

The 1995 and 1996 vintages, especially, are showing themselves to perfection at the present time, with lush apricot, honeysuckle, and juicy, wet honeydew melon fruit and texture. And as sweet and syrupy as this fruit splays itself across your palate, there is an underlying acidity that is brisk and bright in holding all that fruit together, so that it doesn't dissipate itself into caricature.

The '97 is pretty good, too, but needs a little time in bottle yet to fully unfold. The apricot and honeydew are there, with a spritely hint of lime, but the acidity, and an incisive fusel oil component cut into the fruit a bit, for the moment. By Kubrick's 2001 it ought to begin unfolding, showing its true fruit and texture.

Like their dry brethren (or sisters, if you're French), the botrytised Rieslings take age more gracefully than you might expect. In mid 1999 I tasted all the Late Harvest Rieslings, going back to the 1983, which was thick with honey, apricot, caramel, black

walnut meat, baked apple and brown sugar. Dead? Not on your life! Only just beginning to show a bit of tiredness (well earned, one might add). The '89 and '90 were quite lively, with bright Fuji apple in addition to the usual honey, apricot and hints of kiwi fruit. Set any of 'em out with the Roquefort cheese—a superb contrast to so rich a wine—and you'll have a combination to remember and talk about for months.

You must understand that it takes a specific combination of heat and humidity to get this beneficial mold of botrytis going in the vineyard, and these conditions do not crop up with any recognizable regularity. These are wines you simply take when circumstances permit.

"It is a curious thing for a wine we call 'Late Harvest' that we often pick the moldy fruit *before* we pick the unaffected fruit for our regular Riesling," notes Green. "With the botrytis-affected fruit, we pay our pickers by the hour, otherwise they work at a faster pace than we'd like, and they can't do a good job making the evaluation on which clusters to pick. For our Late Harvest, we want only those clusters that are more than half infected by the botrytis mold. We have to demonstrate, beforehand, which clusters we want and which we don't, and we have to monitor the selection process throughout. Fortunately, we're usually working with experienced crews, people who know what we're after, so they make the extra effort to bring in just the right fruit."

He recalls that, in 1997, one acre was left unpicked when the other three acres were harvested for the regular Riesling. "There was no botrytis then developed, and we were gambling that it would. We were lucky. It did. Then you have 1998, which was a very wet year early, but then we hit a hot spell in October that completely dried out the botrytis, so we couldn't make any Late Harvest that year. We're always looking for a way to make some, if there's any way possible."

They even made a Late Harvest Chardonnay one year (1993). Had kind of a burnt apple and honey character. More than drinkable, but lots less than what the Riesling offers with

botrytis.

"You really have to pay attention to the condition of the fruit, with botrytis," instructs Allan. "If you don't pay attention, the fruit goes to raisins very quickly, and you can't get any juice out of a raisin. And it's not like you can accurately random sample botrytised fruit like you can regular fruit. It's guess work, based on your experience and what the weather's doing. It does seem as if we get botrytis more readily in the older Riesling block. Perhaps mold spores have grown into the wood in some way. You'd almost expect to get more in the younger block, which puts out more foliage, has more shade. Doesn't make much sense, in one way."

The Late Harvest usually comes into the winery between 38 and 44 degrees Brix, which makes for thick, sticky-sweet juice. (In fact, the delightfully irreverent Australian diminutive for these wines is "stickies"!) Fermentation typically takes less than a month, but is always completed by spring. "We stop the fermentation at around ten percent alcohol, with residual sugars in the fifteen to twenty percent range," says Green. Even with all that sugar, acidities are right up there, which is what holds all that richness together.

With all that cornucopia of flavor and texture, these are wines that can easily stand by themselves as dessert. If you like contrast, Bleu or Roquefort cheese is ideal, its salty sharpness providing the perfect frame to highlight the richness of the wines. The Late Harvests are also the ideal counterpoints to a ripe honeydew melon or a crusty fruit torte that's not too sweet. Too much sugar in the dessert impinges on the wine's inherent richness, and you don't want to do that. Unless, I suppose, you're an alien. In which case, it doesn't really matter all that much.

# The Tasting Championships

A good deal of wine talk is perniciously precious and pretentious. There is a syrupy arrogance among wine professionals that puts most of us off our feed, and pushes us to a freezer-iced goblet of the *cerveza* instead of a glass of wine when guests arrive.

Allan Green's annual July happening—modestly entitled the California Wine Tasting Championships—offers a pleasant antidote to what I call the "candlelight and caviar" syndrome. Some 400 folks—amateurs and professionals alike—gleefully gather to bask in the summer sun and put their palates on the line in what turns out to be a disarmingly friendly competition. Something of an antidote, as it were, to the deadly serious wine judging circuit, where a winery's reputation is on the line, dependent upon the whims and palates of mismatched tasting panels of winemakers, retailers, wine writers and other pro-

*Lynda Steffen Clark's 1995 Tasting Championships brochure captured the colorful, light-hearted ambiance of the July weekend on Greenwood Ridge.*

fessionals of widely varying skill and experience levels.

(I used to roam the international wine judging circuit, one year judging at 15 competitions from Italy to San Diego, once watching in horror and frustration as the four other members of my *Dallas Morning News* panel refused to vote for a single gold medal among 80 top flight Cabernets, on another occasion witnessing an Italian judge who voted a high mark for a bacteriologically unsound wine so as to, in his words, "encourage the winemaker." To encourage him to do what? I fairly shouted. Continue to make flawed wine? Aieee!)

Originally called the Wine Tasting Olympics, the Championships were started in July 1983. (The word "Olympics" was deleted in the second year at the insistence of U.S. Olympic Committee lawyers but, as Allan likes to point out, "Look who's in trouble now!")

"I always thought that a lot of people—amateurs and professionals, but especially consumers—would really like to see just how their palates stand up, to see if they can recognize a varietal, a vintage, a region, even a winery in a totally blind tasting," says Green. "We set up the Championships to be a fun-filled means of finding out just how sharp someone's sensory perception and memory can be. And, except for the winners, we keep the scores strictly anonymous. You know, in most tastings, it's the tasters judging the wines. Here, in a rather amusing way, the wines judge the tasters!"

The initial press release was cute, urging that the "California Wine Tasting Olympics is an amateur contest for those of us who prefer Riesling to wrestling, and decanting to decathlon." Or, as Allan says, "Something of a 'sporty,' un-serious open house."

The competition was set up in a most straightforward manner. The wines were mainstream California wines—no rare varietals or secret new wineries—and great care was taken to select

*The mood at the Tasting Championships slides between country calm and tasting frenzy. You can tell that the afternoon breeze is already kicking up its heels.*

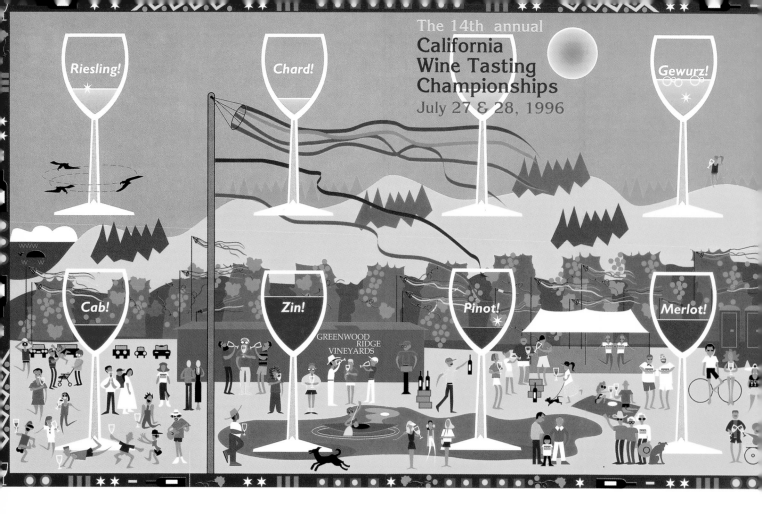

wines that truly represented their variety and appellation, though there are a few 0-for-4 tasters who might question that. "We tried to make sure we didn't have any Zinfandels that tasted like Cabernets," Green says with a sly chuckle. "That wouldn't have been fair." He's also scrupulous in keeping his own wines out of the mix to avoid even the faintest hint of self-promotion. "It's just an opportunity for people to taste and enjoy a series of California wines, and then to encourage comparison and open discussion. That's how we learn best."

In the first round, tasters are simply expected to select the correct grape variety (from a list of eleven) for the eight wines poured. In the final round, there are bonus points for additionally identifying vintage dates, appellations, and then producers. Prizes for the amateur winners at that first Championship (professionals—in production, sales or wine writing—were barred from the initial event) included a weekend for two at the Elk Cove Inn, dinner at the Boonville Hotel, personalized wine tours, and Mendocino County wines.

On the 30th and 31st of July 1983 more than five dozen folks plunked down their hard cash to enter the singles and doubles

94

competitions (you couldn't enter both in those days). Curiously, one of the Doubles winners—he placed second with partner Michael "Flick" MacDonald—was Steve Tylicki. Steve is now the winery's knowledgeable vineyard consultant.

The Singles winner, Ukiah dentist Steve Pasternak, said that he was surprised to win, that he had come only "to have a good time and enjoy myself." Having won, he noted that he had the most trouble with the white wines. "They're a lot more difficult because of the things winemakers do to them. They age them in oak and mask their true flavor!" ("Amen!" quoth the oft-frustrated wine writer.) Pasternak correctly identified three of the four reds poured for him in the finals of the two-day competition, but very nearly whiffed on the four whites, correctly identifying only one of the four varietals. "There were two Chardonnays and one Pinot Blanc, and they were so heavily aged in oak that you couldn't tell them apart! The reds were a little easier. At least there, there's a greater range of color, which offers a clue here and there."

By the second annual Championships, the field had already been expanded to include the present lineup of Novice, Ama-

95

The 15th annual
California
Wine Tasting
Championships
July 26 & 27, 1997

Tasting Answers
Do Not Scratch or Sniff
Before August 1997!

Sauvignon Blanc

White Riesling

Pinot Noir

Gewurztraminer

Chardonnay

Cabernet Sauvignon

Zinfandel

Syrah

The 15th annual
California
Wine Tasting
Championships
July 26 & 27, 1997

teur and Professional categories. Under the spread of white tents and colorful, wind-blown streamers, the previous year's winner, Dr. Pasternak, placed third in the Amateur division. In the Professional division, the *Wine Spectator's* Joe Tarantino won the Singles event, while Calistoga restaurateur Alex Dierkhising (All Seasons Market) and his wine manager Tom Elliot (the reggae musician—huh?—who now owns Northwest Wines) claimed the Doubles crown. "This will certainly add more credibility to our opinions on wine," mused Elliot after the competition. (Rumors that Elliot and Dierkhising were eventually asked, in the gentlest possible manner, to refrain from entering after winning five times in a row are false. "We'd love to have them back," says Green with enthusiasm.)

Tarantino, later writing about the event, captured in a few sentences the essence of the difficulty of blind tasting: "Smells like Petite Sirah . . . but so light colored . . . spicy flavor, but not too rich—Zinfandel. Has to be Zinfandel. But wait, something is not Zinfandel here . . ." Exactly. We call it second guessing, but really it's a question of knowing almost too much, so much so that there's always that next little nuance that throws one off. Which makes it frustrating, which adds humility, which makes it . . . well, fun!

By the mid-'90s, more than 400 people were making their late July pilgrimage to the Ridge to take part in the festive weekend gathering, willing to test their palates and their perceptions against those of others. "It's great to see how this has expanded," Allan told me on the eve of the 1994 Championships. "Last year we had over four hundred people. Some came to compete, some came to picnic by the pond, many were attracted to the chocolate and cheese tasting booths. Some just like our cozy inns, great restaurants, fine wines and splendid scenery."

The Doubles competition is the most fun to watch (and it costs not a *sou* to spectate). It's a kick to see each pair compare notes, discussing the pluses and minuses of their best guesses, and then assessing blame when one or the other has influenced his or her partner into a wrong answer. In 1984 writer/educator Bruce Cass and lab enologist Lisa Van der Water slipped to second place when Bruce persuaded her out of her identification of the 1982 York Creek Petite Sirah as being "too impossible" a scenario. Never mind that Lisa had just tasted the wine at her St. Helena Wine Lab the week before . . . and recognized it again.

In 1985 Gayle Keller, wife and partner of Alex Dierkhising, tied for the Singles crown (with their business partner, Tom Elliot, who else?) by correctly naming Guenoc's 1982 Petite Sirah all the way to appellation, winery and vintage date. Not so easy when you have just four minutes to glean each wine.

One of the most appreciated aspects of the competition is that the wines are unmasked immediately after each round. Partly it's knowing just how well you've done. Partly it's assessing just how far your memory, your breadth of experience and your sensory vocabulary have taken you. Luck plays a part, too. Sometimes, that rare filet mignon aroma doesn't mean Pinot Noir, the apricot is not assuredly Riesling nor the raspberry Zinfandel, the pure black currant isn't Cabernet. And that's what makes it tough. It's not unheard of for contestants to

The 16th annual
California
Wine Tasting
Championships
July 25 & 26, 1998

The 16th annual
California
Wine Tasting
Championships
July 25 & 26, 1998

mutter, as they walk away from their round, "I did pretty good with the crackers!" (The same seems to be true at the chocolate tasting, outdoors under the tent. You have six countries-of-origin to select from with the three samples you taste. For most entrants, it's "I don't know . . . I just entered to eat 'em!")

NBC television covered one of the early competitions, and *Newsweek* magazine has reported on the event. Contestants come from across the country—New York, Connecticut—and even as far away as New Zealand. The more than 400 people who show up each year nearly equal Philo's 470-some-odd population (though only *some* are actually odd).

One year, Green presided over the event in a red-and-white-striped pizza parlor uniform. In 1988 Tom Elliot won the Singles and the Doubles (partnered with Alex Dierkhising, the pair correctly identified the varietals of seven of the eight wines in the final round). In 1990 Sally Siemak won the Amateur tasting, a crown her husband John had previously worn. The tasters had to be particularly adept that year, as Green proffered one red round made up entirely of Zinfandels! (He also confounded the Pros one year when three of the four whites were

*The pond offers a place of serenity to either picnic, snooze . . . or quietly celebrate recognizing the Pinot Noir that everyone else thought was Syrah!*

Chenin Blanc. The dirty rat.) One winner, winemaker Dennis Patton, then-owner of Hidden Cellars (recently purchased by Parducci), is known for riding his bike to the competition all the way from Talmage, south of Ukiah. In 1992, Tom Elliot (this time partnered with Walter Munz) walked away with the top Doubles award for the sixth time in seven tries.

"In the 1997 competition, our Professional Singles winner was Stephen Soltysiak," says Green. "The hospitality manager for Rodney Strong Vineyards [Sonoma County],

The 17th annual
California
Wine Tasting
Championships
July 24 & 25, 1999

Soltysiak identified the grape variety in fifteen of the sixteen wines he tasted! He also earned bonus points for naming the vintage, region, and even the producer of some of the wines. Even more intriguing, is that this is a guy who's really into wine. We recently discovered that his homemade Sauvignon Blanc won "Best of Show" for white wines at the California State Fair's amateur wine competition."

The most recent edition, the 1999 Championships, expanded the venues immensely, offering chocolate (what country is it from?) and cheese tasting contests (separately, not together!), olive oil tasting (you have no idea what range there is in olive oils until you taste a bunch of 'em side-by-side), live blues music by Keeter Stuart and the delectable food stylings of the Boont Berry Farm. Napa's KVON Radio—in the very large persona of Bob "The Wine Authority" Cranston—was again on hand to broadcast the 17th annual wine competition live throughout much of Northern California.

"The tension in the arena is mounting," whispered Cranston to his audience in a voice meant more for an eighteenth hole putt at the Masters in Augusta. The word "arena" only served to make me chuckle, a cartoon vision of lions and Christians came unbidden to my mind.  Cranston, you must understand, is literally a larger-than-life fellow, tall and athletically solid with a voice that can be heard clearly over three states (if you're in New England) and the steely underpinning of, well, *authority*. He clearly adheres to the wine judge/baseball umpire credo, "I may be wrong, but I'm never in doubt."

Cranston embroiders the entry of the Novice competitors: "Look at the fierce look of these warriors.  Oh, watch that elbow to the ribcage, and there's a hip check in the corner!" He's having fun with it, and so are the Novice tasters.  As Allan explains the procedures to the tasters, he reminds them, "It won't really help you to look at your neighbor's scoresheet . . . because he doesn't know what he's doing either."  Which is all too true, as Cranston and I found out tasting along with the Novice tasters.  Bob and I figure the first wine to be a Muscat for its overwhelmingly obvious aromatics.  It's Sauvignon Blanc.  We're dead sure that the second is Chardonnay, with all that oak.  It's Sauvignon Blanc. (Allan's just playing with us.)  Okay, but we've got the third one right. Has to be Gewürztraminer (or at worst, Riesling), what with all that floral, sweet apple spiciness.  Wrong-o. Muscat. (Hey, we got the Zinfandel and the Syrah right.)

Some folks do get 'em right, though.  At this Championships, Stephen Moore of Alexander Valley Vineyards would place second in the Pro Singles, win the Pro Doubles with Kerri O'Brien from Murphy-Goode Winery, then cop the Individual Grand Champion's award.  In the Grand Championship taste-off, where tasters must explain their choices to the audience, Moore correctly and exactly identified a 1994 Acacia Pinot Noir.

It was about that time, as I recall it, that Bob reminded me that, when in doubt, it is usually best to return to Hinkle's First Wine Law.  While it pertains more to the abuse of 100-point scoring systems, which tend to diminish the broad range, depth and individual personality of wines, he is on the right track.

*The Tasting Championships brochures have been drawn since 1995 by Palo Alto's Lynda Steffen Clark, who has also competed every year since 1983. "You can see that Allan appears twice in this one," says Lynda with a laugh. "One of his T-shirts has a monster on it. The other has a monster wearing a T-shirt with Allan on it!"*

That law clearly and non-intimidatingly states that "There are only three categories of wine: 1) I like it; 2) I don't like it; and 3) I'll drink it if someone else pays for it!"

Allan Green eagerly agrees with our anti-precious approach. "I think the great thing about the Championships," he muses, "is that a lot of people who think they don't know a lot about wine will use this as an excuse to come hang out with us for a day or two up here in beautiful Anderson Valley. They enjoy the setting, have a little fun, and most of the time they find out that they know a lot more about wine than they thought they did."

True. But then there are also those timeless moments when they also discover the ringing answer to the following question: When does a Zinfandel taste like a Cabernet? Hah! When you're at the California Wine Tasting Championships. Where else?

But whether you take the tasting seriously or just come to do a modest tune-up on your palate, the event has an ease and a charm that is hard to deny. As one convert wrote recently, "Obviously, people who come are impressed by how much fun they have, and also how inclusive and fair it is. My kids are extremely eager to return, and I didn't have to ask. I also make new friends every visit. I think Brice liked the hay pile the most, and the time when the dog jumped in the pond and swam around."

That is the nice thing about it. There's something for almost everyone.

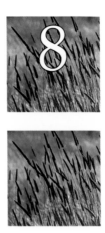

# By Design!

Walking the vineyard, the smell of the ocean just six bird miles away is fresh, pungent, and cleansing. The salt in the air is almost palpable. On an early, crisp morning a hoot owl broadcasts its query, and an echo reverberates down one canyon after another.

Sound—particularly its organized essence, by way of instruments vocal and musical—is an important part of Green's life. Every Thursday evening, between eight and ten, he hosts the local NPR affiliate's program "The Straight Ahead Rock 'n' Roll Show," an ear-opening, deliciously eclectic mix of rock and country and blues and folk and swing . . . and whatever else captures Allan's vivid auditory imagination.

"The station is KZYX & Z in Philo at 90.7 and 91.5 FM," Allan explains. "It's not a particularly strong signal, but it covers Mendocino County pretty well. We started the station in 1989,

and all the programmers are volunteers. A lot of the music I play is pretty obscure, a lot of artists that would otherwise fall between the cracks."

The artists vary. "Well-known blues-rockers that I like include Robert Cray, the late Stevie Ray Vaughan and Bonnie Raitt. On the country rock side, I like Jimmy LaFave, and Lucinda Williams has a great CD out, called 'Car Wheels on a Gravel Road.' Lucinda Williams is the poster child for a new genre that's called 'Americana.' She's hard to categorize, like John Fogerty, whose 'Blue Moon Swamp' is an excellent CD." Hey, *I* know that album! It's what I work out to. Strong beat, off-beat lyrics ("Well, I ain't good lookin' and I ain't so smart, but baby I'm a sensitive guy . . ."), and the same old lyric voice that once drove Creedence Clearwater Revival to such musical heights.

"I've always been a big fan of rockabilly. It's the kind of music that has gotten people back into swing dancing. There are scores of great rockabilly bands these days, like Kim Lenz and her Jaguars, Rosie Flores, Josie Kreuzer, Kenny Love and the Rock-er-fellas; don't get me started, I'll go on and on.

"I play the Grateful Dead but none of that jazzy, weird psyche-delic stuff. And, of course, Ethel and the Shameless Hussies. You don't know Ethel and the Shameless Hussies? Kacey Jones was 'Ethel.' It was something of a Nashville sound, with lyrics that were hilarious. They just disappeared, oh, eight or nine years ago. But they were something!

"The closest thing to them now would have to be the Cornell Hurd Band—my favorite band of the moment. It's almost western swing, but hip and current—also with great tongue-in-cheek lyrics."

The essence of the show is trying to bring something interesting and unusual to outpost Mendocino. "We don't get a chance to hear a lot of new music up here," he says. "It's one of the disadvantages of living up here. I take a lot of flyers on CDs in catalogs and, to be truthful, a lot of it is easily forgettable.

106

It's like panning for gold: You have to sift through lots of mud to find a few nuggets. But then you hear something good, and it really perks your ear up. There was a guitarist, Christine Lakeland, who used to play at the Hopland Brewery. I got a cassette. She was very good, then I didn't hear of her for a long time. She's just turned up again, near San Diego. Someone to keep an ear out for."

## A house and a half

While Allan's sense of the aesthetic is most clearly evoked by his wines, it is also clearly shown by the airy, expansive house his father designed for him in 1994 (Allan moved in just after the crush of '96). "I know what people say, that it's a big house for a bachelor," says Allan with a sly, aw-shucks grin. "But things change, and I'm planning on living here a long time! It reflects the openness of the country here, especially with all

*The view to the west from Allan's house looks toward the vineyard and winery, which is visible in the background.*

*The house is something of a family affair. The house was designed by his father, the ceramics were done by Allan's grandmother, and the table runner was woven by his mother, who also wove the living room upholstery.*

these windows to let the outside in. All the colors and all the materials reflect the ridge, from the slate floor and the concrete fireplace to the redwood columns. It was all built by local craftsmen, orchestrated by Jim Boudoures from Philo Saw Works."

The house was originally inspired by Allan's visit to the Carmel Valley home of his Uncle Charlie, also designed by Aaron Green. "The main things I wanted," explains Allan, "were maximum southern exposure and a good view of the vineyard

*The kitchen is always neat. Allan doesn't cook.*

and winery. Other than that, I wanted it to be fireproof, I wanted a low-maintenance exterior, and maximum sun penetration. I also had a precise layout in mind for my office, just off the kitchen, with my stereo gear on top of the desk, surrounded by shelves for my CDs . . . to make the preparation of my radio show as expeditious as possible."

Still vibrant Aaron Green—who says he especially loves working on projects with his son ("We're working together on a church now; Allan's designing the stained glass windows")—expands on the design aspects: "The house is essentially two long rectangular forms, directly side-by-side and oriented toward the vineyard. The forms seem to be sliding past each other, only to be restrained by the anchoring force of the massive, cast-in-place fireplace. The fireplace is the focus for the expansive interior space that is the result of the intersection of the two linear wings. The roof hovers above, a simple folded plane, held aloft by a rhythmic series of powerfully emphatic wood columns, salvaged from fallen redwood trees found locally."

The senior Green is correct, in that there is a vast sweep to the design that gives the house a lightness, almost as if it were a large egret ready to take flight. A cozy corner off the living room is an arboretum, green with small trees (including Bamboo Palm and Olive Ficus) and plants (Amazon Lily and various *zebrina*) and the wonderful smell of the forest. A dumbwaiter, rescued from San Francisco's Irwin Memorial Blood Bank, transports firewood up from the basement to the soaring living room fireplace that unites the two wings. A modest wine cellar off the guest bedrooms houses future Tasting Championships puzzles and the next room houses Allan's famed beer can collection, now more than 4000 strong.

"When I was going to U.C.L.A.," Allan recounts, "I lived in an apartment surrounded by frat houses. They threw cans in the street, and I started collecting the off brand cans. Later, when I was able to travel a little, I started collecting the foreign brands, and finally joined a beer can collectors club, where I began trading for cans from all over the world. When I found a *can* of vintage-dated, 1964 Les Charmes Beaujolais Supérieur, I began collecting wine cans as well. I used to have the whole collection—when it was much smaller—at the tasting room. But they were getting a little faded by the sun, so now I just have duplicates on display at the tasting room."

Not long ago, Allan discovered three unique wine cans available in an on-line auction. He put in bids on each of the cans, and was quite amazed when even a $330 bid failed to win one of them. On his 50th birthday, he found out who had out-bid him: girlfriend Krisann Kimball had surreptitiously topped his bid by nine dollars. "I initially put in a bid fifty cents higher," she told me with laughter-filled eyes, "but I figured he might guess it was me!" Krisann, who is finishing her degree in occupational therapy, also swings a vicious aluminum bat at the Tuesday night softball games at the fairgrounds.

You can tell a lot about a person by browsing through their bookcases. At Allan's home there are, of course, many books on design concepts and theories, and several titles about the work of Frank Lloyd Wright. Baseball takes up a small corner of Allan's collection, including a well-worn copy of *Joe Morgan: A Life in Baseball*. The inscription on the fly-leaf? "To Aaron— A great guy & a great friend. Joe Morgan. P. S. You're also the world's greatest architect."

## Half a century

In May 1999 Allan Wright Green turned 50. Aside from a grand party—friends had some colorful "Awesome Wine Guy" pins printed up (his initials, you'll note)—reaching the half century mark made Allan eligible to play for the Sonoma County Dirt Dogs, a 50+ hardball team that played in the M.S.B.L. (Mens Senior Baseball League) World Series in Phoenix. Says Allan, the Dirt Dogs' centerfielder/leadoff hitter, "They're a congenial group of guys—no egos out of place, no blame for a blown play—and it's exciting to be playing real baseball again after all those years of softball. I'm one of those people who would much rather *play* than spectate."

Part of "playing" includes an active attention to the environment. In addition to making sure that the vinelands do not intrude upon the land, Allan has always been conscious about the lay of the land itself. "In the mid-eighties, we cut most of the hardwood out of a hundred acres, replanting softwood in an attempt to return the land to what it was like before logging decimated the stands. In three years we planted nearly 25,000 redwood saplings, more than 2,200 Douglas fir, 11,000 Ponderosa pine, and 8000 Sugar pine, those on the warmer, south-facing slopes. Maintaining the land is a constant, on-going process."

As Mendocino County lumber production dips, vineyard income is on a steady rise, and it is predicted that vineyard income will outpace logging income in the next few years. In

*A scene from one of the sumptuous annual dinners created for members of the Advance Tasting Club by Sally Schmitt of The Apple Farm in Philo.*

1998 logging accounted for $126 million, while wine grapes were up from 1990's $40 million, registering a healthy $83 million in 1998. The trend is clear: wine grapes in Mendocino are on a roll.

## Last wines of the millennium

With the decade of the '90s closed, it's easy to see that good winemaking technique is solidly in place. The 1998 Anderson Valley Sauvignon Blanc shows brisk lime, floral grass, green apple and mineral-tight form that begs the fish course. The 1998 Mendocino Ridge/DuPratt Chardonnay is flush with ripe pear, hazelnut, butterscotch, and ripe apple fruit, held together by crusty, French bread aromas that simply tantalize, all of that spread out in a texture that is rich, round, and just lasts inexhaustibly in the mouth.

The Pinot Noir 1998 struts its usual sinful mix of violets,

lavender and dried rose petal aromas, supple in the mouth with a texture that is buttery-plus, with lots of black cherry and sweet leather. The Scherrer Zinfandel of the same vintage is redolent with sandalwood scents, hints of sage, and enough raspberry to immediately transport you to the berry patch.

What to say about the 1997 Mendocino Ridge/Estate Merlot? As much as the bright red currant, cassis, blackberry and sweet tobacco of the fruit charm, it's the texture that elevates this wine to the top of the leader board. Rich and silky at the same time, all that fruit layers itself across your palate to the point that you know you'll have to brush your teeth twice to completely eliminate all that flavor. (I don't recommend that, by the way. Just luxuriate in it. It'll fade away eventually. I think. I'm sure of it.)

## It doesn't hurt that folks like 'em

Mark Bowery, wine consultant to the Albion River Inn and Café Beaujolais and a regular at the Tasting Championships, says, "There's a magic about Allan's wines. They sell like hotcakes! Especially the reds. I think his style appeals to people. The wines are complex and they intrigue."

Greg O'Flynn, founder/proprietor of San Francisco's California Wine Merchants, says with a laugh that it was the alligator on the label that first captured his attention. "But then I tasted the wine, and really liked the Pinot Noir, the Sauvignon Blanc, the Zinfandel, and especially the Merlot. I'm not afraid to pioneer somebody, and most people didn't know about Greenwood Ridge when I first started selling their wines. I started writing up the wines in our newsletter—the Sauvignon Blanc we drank at my daughter's summer birthday party, the perfect wine with its bright, fragrant personality—and people started buying them. A lot."

"The best thing about Allan's wines is that they are each so distinctive," says Peter Marks, a Master of Wine and former wine buyer for Draeger's Markets, who is now a consultant for wine.com. "The Zinfandel has all that dense raspberry

*The winery's designer chocolates, "Eye of the Dragon," are the perfect foil for most any of the red wines.  I like the Merlot with the dark chocolate, the Pinot Noir with the milk chocolate.*

fruit, the Pinot Noir is a personal favorite, and the White Riesling is a most underrated wine, being both delicate and graceful up front, yet possessing the strength to age remarkably well.  It's nice, too, that Allan is such a great guy and such a wonderful host.  I bring my kids up when we do the Tasting Championships, and they have a great old time."

## On chocolate and olive oil

The wild, roaring success of the chocolate tasting every July at the Tasting Championships—along with the success of Mendocino County neighbor John Scharffenberger and his new line of designer chocolates—led Allan to consider his own brand of wine-compatible chocolates.  Finally released in September of 1999, "Eye of the Dragon" (a take-off on the original winery label's lurking alligator) features both a rich dark chocolate (it has the color of delta soil, nearly black) and a lighter, sweeter milk chocolate that simply oozes cocoa.

Allan obviously had a lot of fun designing the package and writing the label copy.  The fire-breathing dragon is the same copper color as the capsules that cover his wine bottles.  And the explanatory copy is a kick.  On the dark chocolate label, "The [cocoa] beans are selectively picked by specially trained left-handed artisans and then roasted to a medium French toast on our proprietary 'Dragonmaster' tongue of flame. . . . DAN-

*From his typical perch on the forklift, Allan inspects Late Harvest Riesling grapes as he dumps them into the hopper. What's unique about this scenario is that these grapes were picked on January 1, 2000. Thus, this will be the first wine of the new millennium!*

GER: Before using this chocolate in combination with Viagra® please raise a toast to the late Wilt Chamberlain." On the milk chocolate label, after a lengthy homily on dragons and distressed damsels, "WARNING: Consumption of this product without the timely accompaniment of Greenwood Ridge Vineyards Zinfandel could greatly inhibit the hedonistic experience." Well, no joke!

"I'm using this name, 'Eye of the Dragon,' as a secondary wine label," says Allan. "We've also got twenty-five olive trees, up by the winery, that might make some pretty good olive oil. It's sure something to think seriously about, don't you think?"

His vineyard consultant, Steve Tylicki, himself an oil expert, agrees. "What makes the Mendocino Ridge area great for grapes—that it's rarely genuinely hot—is also what makes it a good place to grow olive trees for oil. Allan's twenty-five trees were planted in 1997, so it will be a few years yet before they're mature enough to have enough olives for his estate bottled olive oil. I'm monitoring about a hundred trees for three of my Anderson Valley vineyard clients, and there's a fellow in Boonville who has a thousand trees. So it's a happening thing."

## Outpost camp

In the sense of time and transportation, Greenwood Ridge is

certainly a vinous outpost. That makes for a wonderful sense of serenity in an increasingly hyper world that makes outsized virtues of time and accessibility.

Sit up here in the daytime, and you have the classic "hundred-mile view," a sweep of timber and ridgelines and red-tailed hawks lazily seeking elevator thermals. And the night sky is a vast, encompassing bowl of blinking stars that seem, in the endless blackness, almost to extend their reach beneath your feet! An owl screeches off to the right, a coyote howls on your left, and you can, if you listen closely, hear the deer daintily feeding over by that clump of madrone. The forest is chock-a-block full of life. But no alligators.

The great wines of the world cannot be made in proximity to population, mass transit and silicon-driven communication centers. Great wines rely on a strict set of parameters not found just anywhere. The exact amalgam of soil, slope and sun—with the essential evening cooling—are, in fact, fairly rare. The Ridge is one of those places, and even here the good vineland sites are few and far removed, the one from the other.

As the new millennium opens with its multiple aughts (the decade of the aughty aughts?—sorry, but that cracks me up), Greenwood Ridge Vineyards enters its third decade. That, in itself, is a fair measure of success. The real success is wine based, and there the copper capsuled wines shine. The wines of Greenwood Ridge are, in a word, singular. They quietly, but quite clearly, proclaim their regional identity. They are flush with fruit and character and they are refreshing in the mouth, with weight and balance sufficient to virtually demand another taste, another swallow, another bottle. One cannot fairly ask any winemaker to deliver more. Case closed.

# Art Credits

All photography by Kate Kline May except as listed below.

*Cover:* Lynda Steffen Clark
*Back cover:* Wilfried Wietstock
*Inside front flap:* unknown
*Inside back flap, top:* Elizabeth Greene

*Poster:* Martha Anne Booth
*Page 4:* unknown
*6:* unknown
*7 left:* unknown
*7 right:* Allan Green
*14:* Allan Green
*17:* unknown
*20:* Richard Gillette
*21:* George Rose
*22-23:* Richard Gillette
*24 top left:* Robert Franklin
*24 top right:* David Peters
*24 bottom:* Kent Rogers
*29:* Toni Littlejohn
*30:* Nancy Willis
*31:* Nancy Willis
*32:* Wynne Hayakawa
*35 left:* Allan Green
*35 right:* Tom Liden
*38:* Trent Anderson

GREENWOOD RI

GE VINEYARDS